For Nicholas

For if we could be satisfied with anything,
we should have been satisfied long ago.

— Seneca

How to Never Be Enough

Bringing a child into the world without its consent seems unethical. Leaving the womb just seems insane. The womb is nirvana. It's tripping in an eternal orb outside the space-time continuum. It's a warm, wet rave at the center of the earth, but you're the only raver. There's no weird New Age guide. There's no shitty techno. There's only you and the infinite.

I was born two weeks late, because I didn't want to leave the womb. When they finally kicked me out, I was like, *oh hell no.* I've been trying to get back there ever since.

Day one on earth I discovered how to not be enough. According to my mother, the doctor who delivered me said I was pretty. I wanted to believe him, because I love validation. Validation is my main bitch. But I was not the type of infant to absorb a compliment. Had I been verbal I would have extended a compliment in return so as to assuage the implicit guilt of my own existence rubbing up against praise. Instead, I created an external attribution.

An external attribution exists to make you feel

shitty. It's a handy tool, wherein you perceive anything positive that happens to you as a mistake, subjective, and/or never a result of your own goodness. Negative things, alternately, are the objective truth. And they're always your own fault.

The doctor's perspective was only an error of opinion. He obviously had shitty taste in babies. If he'd called me ugly I would have spent the remainder of my time in the hospital trying to convince him I was hot. But he liked me. There was definitely something wrong with him.

If you're never going to be enough, it's important to find a way to turn a compliment against yourself — to reconstruct it into a prison — which is precisely what I did. I decided I would have to stay pretty for the rest of my life. If I got ugly it would be my own fault. Don't drop the ball. Don't fuck it up. I was definitely going to fuck it up.

Next they probably put me in a room with, like, twenty other babies. Immediately, I'm sure I compared myself to all of them and lost. The other babies probably seemed pretty chill about being on earth. They shit their diapers like no big deal. They just sort of effortlessly knew how to do existence. I, on the other hand, was definitely a wreck about being alive. Why was I here? What did it all mean? Things weren't looking good.

My first day on earth and I know I was already thinking about death. A lot. I was probably thinking about death enough to negate every future accomplishment, relationship, and thing that I might come to love with thoughts like *what's the point?* and *why bother?* At the same time, I still can't come to terms with the fact that I am actually, definitely going to die one day, as this might lead to the realization that I might as well enjoy my one brief life, and who wants that.

The situation only got worse when my mother announced that she couldn't breastfeed. More precisely, she told me later, I was "killing her". Killing your mother as an infant is proof of one's too-muchness. In the context of food and consumption, too-muchness translates into not-enoughness: your appetites are too big for the planet, and therefore, you probably shouldn't be here.

I was "killing" my mother, because I was sucking too hard. Less than twenty-four hours on the planet and I was already trying to fill my many insatiable internal holes with external stuff. I was trying to sate the existential fear of *what the fuck is going on here* with milk. I was sucking and sucking, but there wasn't enough milk. There would never be enough milk. One titty is too many and a thousand are never enough. What I really sought was a cosmic titty.

I sought a titty so omniscient it could sate all my holes. The world was already not enough, and I, of course, was not enough either. They gave me a bottle.

As a result of all my sucking, I ended up in a higher weight percentile than my height percentile. This was problematic, because my mother had obese parents. She needed an object upon which to project her own anxieties. I was perfect for that! The religion of the household quickly became food: me not being allowed to have it and me sneaking it.

One of my favorite foods to sneak was me. In an attempt to be enough, I began to consume my own body parts. I ate my fingernails and toenails. I ate every single one. I liked to bite them off and play with them in my mouth, slide the delicious, calcium-rich half moons between my teeth until my gums bled. I tried to enjoy my own earwax, but earwax is an acquired taste. Later in life I became a connoisseur of my own vaginal secretions. The depth of range was astonishing. The vagina is always marinating something.

What I loved most, though, was to pick my nose and eat it. During story hour at school I created a "shield" with my left hand to cover my nose, so I could enjoy some private refreshment. Then I'd really get in there with the right hand. Some of my happiest childhood days were spent behind that handshield. I felt self-contained, satisfied, full on myself. The other kids knew what was up and they made fun of me, but I didn't care. The bliss was too profound.

Unfortunately, the bliss was not going to last forever. Let's be honest, the bliss was going to last four minutes or until my nose ran out of snot. But parents, if your kid is eating herself, you have to let her. Let your child devour herself whole. Even if she disappears completely, encourage her to vanish. Let your child eat the shit out of herself and then shit herself out. Let her eat that.

There aren't that many ways to find comfort in this world. We must take it where we can get it, even in the darkest, most disgusting places. Nobody asks to be born. No one signs a form that says, *You have my permission to make me exist.* Babies are born, because parents feel that they themselves are not enough. So, parents, never condemn us for trying to fill our existential holes, when we are but the fruit of your own vain attempts to fill yours. It's your fault we're here to deal with the void in the first place.

Love in the Time of Chakras

I've had sex with a lot of gross people. I've had sex with enough gross people that I feel like I should have gotten paid for most of them. While I've never gotten paid for having sex with any gross people, I have been a sex worker of sorts.

My first office job was as the administrative assistant of a Tantric sex nonprofit, which we'll call "Electric Yoni". Such places exist, and they exist just north of the Golden Gate Bridge, through the rainbow tunnel, where McMansions meet divination on Highway 1, Marin County, California.

I arrived at the job fresh off four years of psychedelics, deep in woo-woo, talking about energy, the Tao, and telekinesis — believing that an outside fix, an amethyst crystal, the proper measurement of snake oil could save me from myself. Every day I commuted back and forth from my apartment overlooking a crack dealer who swung a golf club in the lower Tenderloin, San Francisco, over that bridge, feeling sort of blessed and sort of miserable.

I was lonely. I had fled the East Coast right

after college in a number of back-and-forth trips, fancying myself as a kind of Jack Kerouac/Hunter S. Thompson/other widely fetishized dude-figure. I was running away from the love of my twenty-one-year-old life, who I broke up with weekly, and was trying to prove to everyone — mostly myself — that I was okay. The psychedelic period had ceased and I was now drinking every day so as not to have to feel what I felt.

Staying drunk seemed like a very practical solution to me. If you could drink yourself into happiness, why would you stay sad and sober? And if you could drink yourself into ultra-happiness, why would you settle for regular happiness?

The first time I saw the Golden Gate Bridge, my ex-love had just come to visit me in San Francisco. At night he was very warm toward me, because we were drunk. We talked about a possible move to the Bay for him. He went down on me to the sound of my housemate's drum and bass (everyone in SF is a DJ) always thrumming from the next room. But during the day, he would be cold and withholding of affection.

After he left, I drove over the Golden Gate Bridge for the first time, alone. I remember the giant mountain moss, rust and rocks, the kind of gargantuan beauty they didn't make back East. I couldn't believe the fairy-tale magnitude of it. I wanted someone to turn to and just go *oh my god*, but I had only myself. I was not enough.

The founder of Electric Yoni, my boss, was a shipping heiress from New York City who had moved to Marin in the eighties in search of something bigger. She had renamed herself Judy Moon. Judy Moon's signature look was anorexic homunculus in spandex. When I arrived, Judy Moon was deep into studying what's known as "nonviolent communication", which she rigorously incorporated into the Electric Yoni course curriculum. But interpersonally, Judy Moon's communication style was still absolutely terrifying. She frequently made hissing sounds. She hissed that my behavior made her feel insecure. All of my behavior.

For years Judy Moon had run Electric Yoni out of her Belvedere mansion, which was 100% pink. The rugs were pink, the walls were pink, the "zafus" for seating were pink. She was known for writhing on the pink floor to demonstrate varying states of Tantric ecstasy (she did this, naked, at our "board of directors" meeting). Eventually, neighbors complained to the local authorities about the blocks and blocks of VW Bugs and Priuses with *Visualize Whirled Peas* bumper stickers jamming up the street. Or perhaps it was the people arriving in various states of undress that bothered them: Renaissance

Fair costumes, medieval bikinis, appropriated Native American dresses, and African dashikis. Whatever it was, the Belvedere rich were finally like, *What the fuck is going on?* So Judy Moon opened a second space — a small center in a neighboring, less ritzy Marin town — where some of the workshops would be held. She called this the Moonrise Center.

Judy felt she had "transcended" from her root chakra to her crown chakra with age. She now sought to expand the course catalog from The Ecstatic Body; 12-Handed Massage; Watsu Rebirthing; Paths of Transcendent Loving; Yoni Yoga; Love Circle; Tantra Levels 1, 2, and 3; and Sacred Dance into a more diverse roster that included Angel Therapy, Life After Death, Reclaiming the Divine Feminine, Anti-Aging Medicine, and of course, Nonviolent Communication.

Through Craigslist, I was hired as an administrative assistant to try to rent out the space of Moonrise Center, to register people for workshops, and to answer all of their questions by phone and email. Judy encouraged me to sample all that the Electric Yoni and Moonrise Center communities had to offer, so that I could better describe "the curriculum".

One of my first experiences engaging in the Electric Yoni oeuvre was to receive a vaginal massage by a man named Jeffrey Kivnik. Jeffrey offered to trade me three hours of vaginal massage in exchange for helping him promote his "practice". Jeffrey was in his fifties and wore a do-rag on his balding white head. I was twenty-one, very pretty, and an active alcoholic and addict. The trade sounded perfect.

I've always had difficulty setting boundaries. And I've always had difficulty reaching orgasm with another human being. So, when faced with an offer to allow Jeffrey to finger me for three hours in exchange for giving him publicity, of course I said yes.

The vaginal massage began with a one-hour full-body massage. Then, for the next two hours, Jeffrey caressed, stroked, kneaded, and tenderized my vagina — or as he called it, my Yoni — using Reiki breathing (I think) so as to aid in the healing of "past vaginal trauma". I never reached orgasm, but I did leave there floating. I think it was the only night in San Francisco that I didn't drink or use drugs.

At the time of Jeffrey's vaginal massage, I had begun dating women. I still slept with cis men occasionally. But I referred to myself as a dyke. Somehow, I convinced one of my lesbian friends to get a vaginal massage from Jeffrey in exchange for her help in promoting him as well. Open-minded and vaguely woo-woo herself, she, too, left Jeffrey's chamber of Yoni floating. But a few days later, she turned to me and said, *I can't believe I let that man touch my vagina.*

Somehow, I also managed to convince my butch, hipster DJ girlfriend to come take a Tantra workshop with me. I can't tell you that I know what Tantra is, even after working at Electric Yoni for a year. But I can tell you what it isn't.

On the pink rug at Judy Moon's Belvedere mansion, ten forty-something single women and five horny men — all Caucasian, and many wearing harem pants — ushered in the new age of sexuality by gazing into each other's eyes and chanting what sounded like *vrom vrom vrom vrom* over and over. Everyone there was seeking. The women, I think, were using sex as a gateway for the love they were seeking. The men, I think, were using love as a gateway for the sex they were seeking. My girlfriend, wearing a newsboy cap and large transparent-framed glasses, was seeking to get out of there. She did the vromming but refused to look me in the eye. I accused her of being unable to try anything new. She accused me of dragging her into a cesspool of hippie filth. We broke up a few weeks later, because I wasn't cool enough for her.

According to *Wikipedia*, "Neotantra or tantric sex is the modern, western variation of tantra often associated with new religious movements. This includes both New Age and modern Western interpretations of traditional Indian and Buddhist tantra. Some of its proponents refer to ancient and traditional texts and principles [vromming?], and many others use tantra as a catch-all phrase for 'sacred sexuality,' and may incorporate unorthodox practices...

"As tantric practice became known in western culture, which has escalated since the 1960s, it has become identified with its sexual methods in the West. Consequently, its essential nature as a spiritual practice is often overlooked. The roles of sexuality in tantra and in neotantra, while related, are actually quite different."

The trouble with sublimating the desire for love and sex into a watered-down, reappropriated version of ancient wisdom is that sometimes shit goes down.

I was both proud and ashamed of my job at Electric Yoni. On the one hand, it felt good to be supporting myself. At the same time, when I told my parents where I worked, my father googled it from his office and asked me why the website was blocked for sexual content.

I met a man named Mamadou while looking for bigger spaces in which to hold our yearly roundup of teachers — a buffet of Tantra, if you will — which always drew the biggest crowd. Mamadou was a soft-spoken man in his sixties who ran a local religious center at the top of a beautiful mountain. We talked of the poets Hafiz and Rumi. He told me that he really liked being with me and asked if I would come visit him at the center again, perhaps on the weekend for lunch. I said okay. Then he asked if I could bring weed and coke.

Mamadou said that not only would he pay for the coke and weed, but he would also pay just to spend time with me. He said a girl like me deserved to be earning more than I was earning at Electric Yoni. Despite the request for drugs, Mamadou seemed so centered, so spiritual, so into my thoughts on Rumi, that I didn't imagine there was anything sexual about the request.

That Saturday I went bearing the coke and weed. Mamadou gave me $700 up front — $200 for the drugs and $500 for my time. Then he poured big glasses of red wine and served a series of beautiful Persian dishes: some kind of lamb, a vegetable dish, a sweet casserole. We ate and got drunk. Mamadou showed me pictures of himself from his youth. He had actually been handsome. He told me that he was bored of his life now. His spirit sought more fun. He asked if it would be possible that I come back weekly. He would give me $500 each time, plus money for drugs. Now I would really be financially self-sufficient.

The next time I came back it was more of the same: the weed, the wine, the coke, the delicious Persian dishes. But then he put his hands on my waist. Then his face came in for my mouth. I was like, *No fucking way.* Mamadou was like, *Darling. You didn't think I enjoyed your company that much, did you?* I left with my $700 and never went back.

Why didn't I have sex with Mamadou? Why didn't I have sex with him regularly and get paid? He was old and unattractive, but unattractive hadn't stopped me during my run in San Francisco. There were 300-pound men and acorn penises I had sex with for free. There was a karaoke DJ who verbally abused me for not liking Tom Waits. He never bought me shit. There was a bartender with a bowl cut who I don't remember sleeping with, but when I saw the used condom on the windowsill the next morning and looked at him inquisitively, he said, *You were a disaster. You cried the whole time.* When you're lonely and blacking out in strange places, you let other lonely people do what they want to you. You call it free love.

Ultimately, I think I didn't sleep with Mamadou because I wanted to believe that somebody would pay $500 for my personality. Free love sounds so beautiful. I have always fetishized the sixties. But something tells me that free love was a lot easier emotionally for the men — when they could actually get some — than the women.

I know that in her quest for the divine orgasm, Judy Moon had been hurt over and over by men. They had used her for her money, concealed their homosexuality, refused to become a primary partner (the equivalent of "he just can't commit" in the polyamory community).

One time, on a spiritual hike, she stopped hissing for a moment to tell me that she was a second mother to me and wanted me to consider her as such. I looked at her like, *Bitch, are you crazy?* But it was also sad to me — that someone who taught legions of women how to access the divine goddess had such a lack of understanding for what the love between two women could be. It was also sad that Judy believed she could simply say she was my second mother and I would believe it. Like she could do it in an affirmation. I was far from home. I needed a second mother. But I wasn't that needy.

I lasted a year at Electric Yoni. After that I got an internship at a hipster magazine in San Francisco, but any sense of workplace boundaries I may have possessed had been decimated. Two weeks into the internship I was let go for hugging the publisher, instead of shaking hands, in front of a primary advertiser. The publisher never explicitly told me what I had done wrong, but as soon as I came out of the embrace I knew it was bad. I judged myself for it.

Shortly thereafter I returned to the East Coast, where I continued to fuck around for the next year and a half, before getting sober. I blacked out in stairwells and taxis, tried to have sex with gay men, woke up with strangers and mysterious blood on the wall — just as I had done in San Francisco. I was still melting down. But New York — unlike San Francisco — had a stable ground on which to hit bottom.

I Want to Be a Whole Person but Really Thin

I am an eater of numbers. I prefer packaged foods, foods with a bar code, because they make the math simpler in counting calories and that gives me a sense of peace. It's just an illusion of control, really, but that illusion is everything. It makes me feel safe. It gives me a stillness in my mind. All I've ever wanted is peace.

I am a vanity eater, a machinelike eater, a suppresser-of-feels eater. I save the bulk of my calories for the end of the day so that I have something sweet and seemingly unlimited to look forward to. I do not trust the universe to provide enough of anything to fill my apparently bottomless hunger. That's the case with my consumption of a whole pint of diet ice cream with six packets of Equal poured into it every single night. It's a way of offering myself something cloyingly saccharine and seemingly infinite. I don't believe that the world, or god, will give me that sweetness. So I am giving it to myself. I am going to bed full of sweetness that the day may not have provided. And I am defeating the laws of nature by doing this with diet ice cream. Most nights I would rather curl up with the diet ice cream than be in the world.

I am an eater who enjoys structured magic. I don't feel courageous enough to let myself eat whatever I want, because I don't want to face the wrath of what my mind will do to me after. I have a vested interest in keeping things under control, because when I lose my illusions of control I get very scared. The world is scary enough as it is. Just let me have this way of life. Let me continue to live under these self-imposed systems of diet ice cream, where I can have some of what I enjoy about binge eating — just without my mind destroying me after.

I am an eater who doesn't trust herself. I am a bad mommy to myself and a poor steward of my body. I am an eater of rituals and a ritualistic eater, an eater who knows better but sees no impetus to get better because this kind of works and I feel more secure in my body at this weight.

I am an eater who is playing a game that mostly exists in my head but has also been curated by various social cues, including those from my mother.

I am an eater who was born two weeks late, in a higher weight range than my height range. My mother was terrified that I was going to be fat (her parents were both obese, though she herself is of "normal" weight). She restricted and controlled all morsels that I put in my mouth when in her presence. She threatened to ask teachers and camp counselors what I was eating. She asked, *Do you want to be a chubbette or do you want boys to like you?*

I am an eater who was not allowed cake at birthday parties. I attended Hebrew school, but the religion of the household was food. My father aided in the sneaking of food. He took me to the park as a toddler and snuck me my first giant cookie. A Canadian goose stole it out of my hand. He took my sister and me on trips without my mother and packed the backseat of the car full of junk food. My grandmom Eve took us for weekends and fed us the whole time: mini bagels, pigs in a blanket, candy cigarettes, licorice pipes. I stole food from other kids' lunches, then tried to trade them their own food for more food.

I am an eater who binge ate regularly as a child. One favorite was a bagel with mayonnaise or cream cheese and then cheese melted on top. I stole change from my mother's "library fund" (she was an inner-city school librarian) and used it to order pizzas and sandwiches. I bought candy at the gas station near school: Milky Way, 3 Musketeers, Twizzlers, Heath bars. I hoarded the wrappers, then tried to flush them down the toilet. They clogged the toilet and I was discovered.

I am an eater who went away for the summer to a coed camp (up until this point I attended an all-girls school and a camp where boys were across the lake). It was easier to diet when there were boys around. The payoff was right there. So I restricted my food intake. I grew three inches. I got a tan. I was fourteen. A sixteen-year-old with vodka on his breath said I was beautiful. We Frenched and he touched my tits. He was my boyfriend. At night he fucked a counselor. A lot of boys got crushes on me. I dated five of them in a row. My parents came for visiting day and my mother freaked out with joy at how thin I was. I got my period. I got my boobs. Boys continued to like me. They came and went. I alternated between restricting and bingeing heavily on food.

I am an eater who got into a car accident with my father's car because I was pouring artificial sweetener into a container of cottage cheese and ran a red light. The air bags exploded and I broke my arm. I was sixteen and began heavily restricting my food intake. I went on a fat-free-muffin diet: one muffin in the morning, one muffin in the afternoon, chicken for dinner. I got the boyfriend of my dreams.

Over time, I became severely anorexic. The muffins turned into apples. I was five foot five and weighed 101 pounds. I stopped getting my period. I froze. I grew fur. My father felt he couldn't say anything. My teachers were concerned. My mother thought I was fine until I told her I stopped getting my period. This scared her (she wanted grandchildren someday). She sent me to a nutritionist and a therapist. It didn't really work. I only ate packaged foods so that I knew the caloric content. I began adding calories and slowly recovered physically.

I am an eater who went to college very underweight. I discovered weed and booze. I began bingeing and couldn't stop. All the foods I hadn't eaten throughout my anorexia were suddenly mine again: pancakes, pizza, Taco Bell, chocolates, gummy candies, General Tso's chicken, cookies, ice cream with cereal on top, nachos. I gained fifty pounds.

I am an eater who began taking amphetamines daily. Ecstasy, too. I ran and worked out a lot on ecstasy. I got into laxatives — the chocolate ones. My weight "regulated". I moved to San Francisco, where I dieted during the week and took laxatives every day and binged on weekends. I couldn't make myself throw up. I once tried ipecac syrup and puked martinis and Indian food all night. That night was a boyfriend's going-away party. I didn't show up or text.

I am an eater who somehow became a normal eater from ages twenty-five to twenty-nine. I still thought about food and worried about weight a lot. A retired baseball player doesn't stop thinking about the game. But it was the healthiest I had ever been. I think what made my eating more "normal" at this time was that I had just gotten clean and sober. I was no longer drunkenly bingeing on food. The munchies were gone. I was no longer using amphetamines to starve. The calories I'd ingested from alcohol in the past were now freed up for actual food.

I also remember, having been fucked up every day for years, that the world seemed like such a novelty to me during my first few years sober. Like, I remember going through each of the seasons and the magic of rediscovering what it felt like to be in the world: going to a pumpkin patch on Halloween, getting a tree for Christmas. I felt excited by reality in a way that I never had before. I actually wanted to be alive. I wanted to sample what the world had to offer, and this included food.

I am an eater who refuses to be the kind of woman who "lets herself go". I got married at twenty-nine and noticed that I was gaining some weight. I panicked that I would soon become amorphous, lose my independence, sexual appeal, and maidenhood — like the weight that was accumulating on my belly and thighs was a symbol of the blurring of my identity. Where did I begin and end? Rather than asking myself these questions, I went on Weight Watchers.

Weight Watchers points is a beautiful system

for someone who is absentminded about food. They aren't the greatest for someone who has had eating disorders all her life. The world became numbers to me and I was doing more math than I ever had before. I got off Weight Watchers and went back to just counting calories. The world became different kinds of numbers, the old, familiar kind. This is how I eat now. The world is still numbers, but it is algebra, not calculus.

I am an eater who is a horrible feminist, probably. I dream of what I would eat if I identified as a man and it looks vastly different from what I eat as a woman. There would be so much pizza. The Mountain Dew would runneth over and it wouldn't even be diet. If I do not believe that I as a woman deserve pizza, what does that say of my views of other women? If I do not love my body, how can I love the body of any other woman? I could say "I love my body" so that I appear to be a good feminist. But that only means pretending to love something I hate.

But I am an eater who is a good feminist, maybe, because I am being honest with you now. I am telling you the truth: that I have not yet dismantled the many warped schemas that define the way I see my body and the bodies of other women. I am giving you permission to tell the truth about where you are in your process of dismantling your fucked-up schemas.

I am not pressuring you to dismantle anything. I am saying let's be here together, undismantled, and just accept that this is where we are. Let's love each other right where we are, even as we compare ourselves to one another. I am saying, yes, baby, I know it's hard.

But I am an eater who is a hypocritical feminist. I lust the body I do not allow myself. I lust the zaftig female body. The women I am most sexually attracted to are considered obese by today's (and yesterday's) standards. I don't watch a lot of porn, but a typical search term for me is "fat lesbians". What a beautiful fantasy: to be accepted and embraced and adored as your biggest self, the most you, by a woman who is her fullest her. To gorge together, uncontrollably, with no need for limits — and then to devour one another — to lick and hump and rest in the acceptance of each other in your grandest *is*ness. That, to me, is freedom. The ultimate letting go. It's sexy as fuck. It really turns me on. I want to let go all the way, but it's a freedom I cannot allow myself in my daily life. Is this feminism or is it just desire and objectification?

But I am an eater who is the worst feminist, probably, because I objectify other women. I compare my body to the bodies of other women. Occasionally, I win. What does it mean to win? It means that my body fits more closely to the bodies of the models in magazines on which I grew up. It means that I am skinnier. It means that I am in some way beyond reproach, or further from reproach. I am terrified of reproach. But reproach from whom? Who is the voice of the reproacher? Does it even exist? Is anyone beyond reproach?

I am an eater who feels safest at a place of very thin. I want to live in a body that is so far away from being fat that it has room to gain weight and still not even rub elbows with chubbiness. Fat, for me, in terms of my own body, represents terrible feelings: shame, disintegration, self-hatred. These are feelings that I experienced as a child and want to protect myself from feeling ever again (though that is, of course, impossible and I feel them every day in whatever body I have).

I am an eater who still longs, sometimes, for the full binge. There were moments in my life when I was mid-binge that felt like some beautiful return to self. I would be so caught up in the flow of the action, the pure pleasure of no restrictions and uncontainability, that I felt as though I had entered a silence that existed before words. But the words always returned. They were in my head and they yelled at me.

What was that silence? Was it the spiritual space of true freedom? Or was it simply another coping mechanism — food as a drug — to block out the world? Is it my true self to eat until my stomach can hold no more and I am repulsed by the sight of any more food and I cannot do anything but lie in the fetal position and groan? Or is that a reaction to restrictions that were placed — first by others, then by me — on some other true self? Is there a part of me that knows how to feed herself enough, only what she loves and what nourishes her, and never feel shame or fear if she overindulges a little, because it tastes so good? Did that part of me never exist and must be manifested? Or did it always exist, as it does for the animals, but along the way got buried? How would I even begin to uncover it?

I am an eater who knows, intellectually, that control is an illusion. I know it experientially and spiritually, through peak experiences and gentle experiences and love and sudden pain and tragedy. But asking the mind to give up control and the mind actually obeying is another animal.

I am an eater whose mind says no.

I am an eater who knows that ultimately you are responsible for yourself, an eater who doesn't want to take responsibility for herself other than to seek the feeling of safety.

I am an eater who is scared to be so honest here, a disordered eater.

I am a superficial woman of depth.

Help Me Not Be
a Human Being

My sexual preference is me. Actually, escaping me. In every obsession, Internet obsession, make-out, fuck, and actual relationship, I've embraced my fellow man (and woman) on the highway of low self-esteem in the hope that I could be convinced of my own okayness and/or disappear.

What I have sought in love is a reprieve from the itch of consciousness — to transcend myself and my human imperfections — but this has yet to happen. What has happened, instead, is a lifetime of fictional love stories; fiction, in that I have perceived every new experience through the veil of my own insecurities. Here are some of those stories.

I'm in love with you and you don't want anything to do with me so I think we can make this work: a love story.

Just saw two ants drown together in my bathtub and it reminded me of us: a love story.

The saddest part of fucking you in that motel room was not when you took a shit in the bathroom before we fucked and not when I had to put on

Tupac to mask the sound of you shitting and not when the smell leaked out into the hotel room and not when I licked behind your balls after you took that shit, even though you hadn't showered (I don't care, to be honest. I think that germs have kept me healthy and strong my whole life. It was only when I told my friend the story and she called me out on it that I realized my disregard for my own personal health might be indicative of a deep self-hatred.), but when I went into the bathroom an hour after you took the shit and there were still shit marks in the toilet bowl and I thought about how if it had been me who took the shit I would have absolutely gone into that toilet bowl with my bare hand and a piece of toilet paper and wiped it down and how maybe this particular brand of self-consciousness regarding shit marks is a developmental variation in response to the fundamental differences in expectations placed upon men vs. women in this society, though that's probably too reductive: a love story.

That's not the clitoris: a love story.

The anxiety of the sexual act is my sexual act: a love story.

Definitely thought I was a lesbian until we dated and then I thought I might just be asexual, or not asexual, actually, but even more deeply fucked up than I ever knew: a love story.

I never liked myself: a love story.

Sorry I fell asleep while you were going down on me: a love story.

One night I dreamt you had a gherkin instead of a penis and when I saw you at work the next day I thought I was in love with you (the thing about spending eight consecutive hours in a confined space with the same people day after day is there will always be that one person who appears more special and attractive than he or she actually is), so when we ended up having sex on three different occasions I said *never again* after each time, though when you licked my ass it felt so intimate that it made me want to buy you beautiful shirts, and when I asked you if you would ever want to be with me for real (if I didn't already have a boyfriend) you said yes (but it's easy to say yes when the other person is already taken): a love story.

I wanted to build a fire with our shadow selves and burn there or be erased by the narcotic of limerence when I turned your face into a fire: a love story.

I don't even masturbate to you anymore because it's too sad: a love story.

My therapist calls you pancake ass: a love story.

It's not that I'm shutting you out when we have sex, I just need to fantasize about obese women caring for one another's vaginas to have a good orgasm and you're a midsize man: a love story.

Just because you have beautiful eyes doesn't mean you're deep: a love story.

When you said, *Don't obsess, just feel the feelings*, I said no: a love story.

Sorry you are having a really good life and are contented by it: a love story.

I don't want to be older and wiser, I want to be younger and hotter: a love story.

In the dark you looked so human in your skin that I called you *human* in my head and didn't want you then and felt relieved: a love story.

When you said that your sexual ideal is romantic sex where both partners say *I love you* as they are coming, and then do that with a different person every day, I totally agreed except I only wanted to do it with you: a love story.

I feel like my life has a lot of caves and they are all filled with your hair: a love story.

Let's pretend you are capable of being who I think I need you to be: a love story.

When you tweeted that the best you could ever arrive at is probably the leader of a sex cult, I guess I should have seen that as a red flag: a love story.

Well, I was clearly more into that than you were: a love story.

I think it's time for you to drop back into my life, ruin it, then disappear again: a love story.

The best part of fucking you in that bathroom at the Rivington Hotel was when I went to Sephora first and did my makeup using all their testers for free, especially the Yves Saint Laurent lip lacquer. P.S. When you said, *Let's fuck at the Rivington Hotel*, I thought you meant you were getting an actual room: a love story.

I'm sorry that when you asked what you could do to help me have an orgasm I said *leave the room*: a love story.

Sometimes when I need to comfort myself (all the time) I think about your lisp and it creates a wombskin around my brain full of barbituratesque nectar, the side effects of which include a horny surge in my second chakra and pussy, and then severe withdrawal: a love story.

The man just wanted to put his dick in things and the woman wanted her pussy to be perfect: a love story.

I only had sex with you to get you to stop talking about your art: a love story.

Wish I had a dick too: a love story.

I never really liked you but everyone else was worse: a love story.

Secretly it hurt my feelings when you were outed

as a sexual predator, because for me you couldn't even get it up: a love story.

I've been on your FB page for five hours today: a love story.

Imagining that you are going to come back to me is my favorite way to spend the day: a love story.

I still can't believe that someone as hot as you has validation issues but I also know that being a very sensitive person on this planet is painful and some of us are built like sieves, or have holes where any external validation just pours right through and we never get full, and I also know it's ultimately an inside job anyway and no amount of external validation will ever be enough (though damn it can feel good in the moment, and it sort of makes me mad at god, actually, like, okay god, you built me like this so teach me how to validate myself in a way that feels as good as when a boy does it or the Internet does it, because there is always a cost when a boy does it or when the Internet does it): a love story.

Yeah, all my orgasms were fake: a love story.

We're going to spend the rest of our lives together in my head: a love story.

When I send nudes I like to receive a full dissertation on their greatness: a love story.

Remember when I yelled out *I just want to eat*

pussy! in your car and you said I might actually be a real lesbian and then I ate your pussy better than a real lesbian but was still only bisexual: a love story.

I pretended you were this blond girl named Kirsten every time we had sex for two years: a love story.

I don't want to get off the Internet or consider anyone else's needs: a love story.

I miss the sex that I thought was love, but you knew was just sex: a love story.

The worst was when I tried to get revenge for having had a crush on you in high school and you not wanting me, because I got a lot hotter after high school, so I made a plan and the plan was that you would want me and I would kiss you but not sleep with you, yet somehow by the end of the night I ended up begging to suck your dick: a love story.

Tell me if I'm texting too much: a love story.

No teeth on the clit, thanks: a love story.

I thought we were good for each other, but my friends said you were crazy, and I don't really trust my taste in people (or in anything, actually, and there's good reason for that) so goodbye: a love story.

Sorry we couldn't get it in my ass: a love story.

You said spirituality couldn't be bought but I felt really holy eating egg salad sandwiches in your apartment: a love story.

The G-spot isn't where you thought it was: a love story.

When you said you just wanted it to be a one-night thing, I kinda hoped you meant one night over and over and over until we die: a love story.

I guess you aren't going to rescue me from my life: a love story.

Text me back: a love story.

Love Like You Are Trying to Fill an Insatiable Spiritual Hole with Another Person Who Will Suffocate in There

I tell myself I know nothing about love so I can recover. I am recovering from a fantasy that I projected on a young man's body. He provided music and language and fingers and a face that moaned into my pussy. I am never going to recover from being that alive.

I was in love with him. I don't care that well-meaning people tell me it was lust or infatuation, though I have started saying it was lust or infatuation so as not to be called out first by well-meaning people. Well-meaning people can save me from myself, but they cannot save me from being alive. Only my god can do that. Sometimes my god speaks through well-meaning people. Sometimes I am so lonely.

love (noun) — a feeling of strong or constant affection for a person (Merriam-Webster online dictionary)

Was it love when we met on the Internet? Was it love when he pursued me with silly messages and praise for my writing and a picture drawn in my favorite candy? When an attractive person pursues you, there is the luxury of not having to worry about whether it is love, because you are not the one doing the pursuing. At least, not at first. My usual habit of falling for people, when I think I am not falling, seemed irrelevant. He poked and messaged and "liked" and faved my every Internet itch. I had my feelings, any feelings, under control.

love (noun) — attraction that includes sexual desire: the strong affection felt by people who have a romantic relationship (*Merriam-Webster* online dictionary)

lust (noun) — intense sexual desire or appetite (Dictionary.com)

I was the one who escalated it. I was the one who made it overtly sexual, as I get nervous in undefined spaces and feel compelled to sexualize things. One day we were messaging about my favorite cereals (Kashi GoLean, Cocoa Krispies post-milk). Then we were messaging about his stomach issues, which I called his "poop game", as in "how is your poop game?" He said it was hard to talk about his poop game with anyone he hadn't been inside. But once he was inside a person, the poop memoirs could just flow. I asked him if he wanted to be inside me. He said *yeah!!!!* Then he asked if I was being for real. I messaged him my number. I said we could play the sext game. We sexted all afternoon.

Him: I want to fuck you in an air duct, flattened out with our whole bodies touching, at first slow and careful, then really hard until I come in you and the bottom of the duct falls out and we fall into a boardroom meeting for walmart, like into a bucket of fondue

Him: Also eat your pussy

Me: slow and then hard is good fucking. I want to look at yr pretty face while you fuck me and I want it to look like you are on some other shit. I want you to moan in my mouth

Him: I want to whisper in your mouth that I want to fuck you while I'm already fucking you

Him: I want to peel off your tights real slow while watching your face and push you onto a bed and go right for one really long, slow lick from the bottom of your pussy all the way to right before your clit, and even slower, trace it lightly with my tongue

Me: lol tights

Me: that's v good. i want to hear you say my

fucking name and look me in the eyes as I lick the head of your cock, suck the shaft and lick yr balls so slow it kills you

Me: I want you to tease my belly, pussy and thighs until I am begging

Him: Mmmm I want to feel myself about to come and grab the back of your hair in a bunch and ease your mouth back and forth on my cock with full, long strokes until I come in your mouth while I watch you watch my eyes

Me: you will know how much I am enjoying sucking yr cock w my wet mouth bc I will be moaning on it.

Him: Yeah fuck I want to feel your moans on my cock

Him: I want you to rub your pussy under your waistband while you suck my cock through my jorts

Him: Lol lol

Me: I want you to tell me how bad you want to make me come and to take as long as I need. then I want you to lick my little pink clit so fast and gentle like yr tongue is my personal vibrator while I surf the internet. 10 minutes after I tweet, delete that tweet and then tweet another tweet I come in yr mouth

Him: I want to fave your tweet as you come

around my face, which is soaked with your pussy juices

Him: I want to rt while you hold my head against your clit during your last cum clenches

Me: I want u to @ me while you lick my clit. then as I come I will say yr name over and over and respond to yr @ that way b/c I don't @ on twitter and everyone knows that

Me: as i am cumming i want you to put yr fingers inside me to feel my muscles moving but not before. that will be yr response to my response to yr @

Me: fyi, I will lick you behind yr balls like I am eating the most delicious pussy

Him: I want to go deep in your Twitter feed and fave an unfaved tweet as a means of communicating that 1. I respect your art and love your pristine feed and 2. That I like getting the @ reply way better this way

Me: I keep my pussy even more pristine than I keep my feed

Me: I will like 3 of yr statuses on fb while I swallow yr cum

Him: I'm gonna eat it and get so sick and die due to its being too pristine for my human body to process, but I'll come back as a ghost and finish the job

Him: I'm going to finger your wet pussy with my middle finger while I cum in your mouth and with my left hand share a poem you posted with the caption: soo good

Him: I'll lick your clit for 127 hours

Me: I will like yr share of my poem with one hand and hold yr wrists down w the other as I fuck you on top. I'll be kissing yr mouth as I do this

Me: I want you to tell me how badly u want to taste me after you've already been licking it. this shld happen at the 121st hour

Him: I'm going to fade in and out of a physical nirvana dimension due to length of my eating your pussy, my cock getting so hard that it cuts through spacetime and fucks our common ancestor

Him: I want to print out a screenshot of "Melissa Broder likes this" and come on it

Me: I want u to take a picture of yr cum on the screenshot of "Melissa Broder likes this" and send it to me. and I want it signed by the cummer.

Him: God I want to fuck you in a treehouse and have someone's parents find us and instead of stopping speed up and fuck each other as hard and fast as we can until we come and when we wake up they've died from shock! Sad

Him: I'll sign it w my cum

Me: I will write a poem abt yr face as I watch it go in and out of tangible reality while u eat my pussy for 127 hrs and it will possess themes of the succubus, the transcendent and temporal angst and it will be the worst poem I ever wrote

Him: want to fuck you from behind and squeeze your asscheeks until you spit out your next chapbook whole and we watch it get railed by a hot nyt reviewer coed

Me: I want to tell you "i embrace your shitgame" while you are fucking me next to their dead bodies and say "even if you had to shit at this very moment I wld not judge you, u cld just shit, just shit everywhere, and it might even turn me on, even though shit has never been my thing — not that there is anything wrong with ppl who are into it — but the intimacy of the act, yr powerlessness over it and my delight at my own radical acceptance wld be hot" and then instead of shitting you come really hard

Him: ~The perfect sext~

Him: U did it

We continued like this for a year, never meeting IRL for the first six months. He lived in DC and I was in New York, then Los Angeles. We explored various tropes along the way, from the crucifixion (**Me:** *can u tease my pussy over my undies in an amphitheater from like 31–33 AD then finger me in a dark alley while jesus is crucified and like not know he is getting crucified bc i am dryhumping u against a wall* / **Him:** *Can you suck your pussy juice off my fingers at the exact moment our Lord and Savior rises, and he sees you sucking my fingers and goes "hold on" and stops rising, but then goes "jk" and rises again, and everyone laughs*) to the Arctic (**Him:** *Touching my cock, thinking about you kneeling over it, dropping yourself slowly onto me, on a beautiful glacier* / **Me:** *there is a sephora on the glacier and my lips are unnaturally red* / **Me:** *i lick the head of yr cock through the galactic gloryhole, french kiss it slowly outside the timespace continuum* / **Him:** *My cock glows an incredible iridescence as I enter you. The warmth of your pussy against the cold night creates a clap of thunder between us, somehow* / **Him:** *We set off a nuclear reaction in your pussy, each of us coming to the other's throbbing orgasm*).

We also texted about other things: depression and anxiety, therapy sessions, the hamster wheel of the mind, our secret childhood pains, what it might mean to have a second childhood, different types of voids, a bad acid trip involving the moon. We sent pictures of our naked bodies. He told me that a poem he'd written, which I'd admired, he'd written for me. No one had ever made me the muse before. Something inside me shifted. The little kid in me erupted. She said, *You see me. I am finally seen.*

It takes so little, really. How well do we see someone who we know only for a brief while? How well do we ever see anyone at all? I know too much and I know nothing at all.

infatuation (noun) — an object of extravagant, short-lived passion (The American Heritage Dictionary of the English Language, fourth edition)

The first time we met was at a hotel in the financial district in Manhattan, just before Thanksgiving. I remember sitting on the hotel toilet, trying to make myself shit before he got there. He seemed to have had a lot of anal. I, nine years older than him, had never had anal. I enjoyed cleaning myself, making myself look beautiful, dressing for him.

When he arrived in the hotel room, I thought *Jesus*. He had the black hair of a pixie, the face and body of a gazelle. I was relieved that he passed for normal. Hot-normal. People on the Internet often get weirder and less attractive when you get offline. I remember we hugged for a long time, as if to say, *I know you*. We sort of did know each other.

Also, not at all. Then we started kissing. I remember his lips were chapped. I remember feeling like the kisses were too hard. It felt like a forced urgency, and despite his assurances that he would eat my pussy infinitely, I didn't think there was any way my body could catch up. It felt cinematic in a bad way. After all the sexting we both had too much to live up to.

Next we were in our underwear, rolling around on the hotel bed. I wanted to rewind and start again, to move in slow motion. He licked my pussy and I found myself faking or at least moaning in a dramatic way — something I had done with other lovers in the past, when my brain and body were nowhere near the pace but I wanted to seem present. I think I tried to suck his dick to space things out. I think I tried to get him hard. He must have felt the way I did, because he stayed soft.

Then I think we were making out again on the bed. Suddenly, I felt a wave of all of the sadness and all of the fear that I usually keep dammed up. I drowned for a minute. I felt like he could feel it. What I didn't consider at the time was that the sadness could have been coming from him. Later he apologized for what he called a dark energy that he had brought with him — a depressive state that he couldn't shake that night. But I thought it was my own. Maybe it was both of ours, and maybe it was what bonded us to each other underneath all of the sexting. I think we were both looking for light, maybe a fake light, maybe a real one.

I said, *You have experienced a lot of pain in your life. You are so intuitive.* I didn't tell him that I felt like he could intuit my own historic pain in that moment.

He told me he was getting tired. Would I mind if he slept some? I told him, *Of course not,* but felt rejected. I realized I hadn't eaten in many hours. I told him I was going to go out for food and asked if he wanted anything. He said no. I wondered if he was hesitant to eat at sleepover situations because of his digestive issues.

I went to 7-Eleven and bought a thousand calories worth of food: a Golden Grahams bar, a pack of M&M's, some weird Japanese-looking peanut-butter-and-jelly sandwich. Back at the hotel room, I sat on the bed feeling really cute and pretty. I ate, mindful of him, like I was putting on a show. I told him that he should sleep and that I was going to take the second big bed (there were two).

love (noun) — a deep, tender, ineffable feeling of affection and solicitude toward a person, such as that arising from kinship, recognition of attractive qualities, or a sense of underlying oneness (The

American Heritage Dictionary of the English Language, fourth edition)

I don't remember drifting off but I remember waking up at dawn the next morning and brushing my teeth, then getting back into bed, pretending to be asleep. I heard him get up to brush his teeth. I heard him piss. I opened my eyes and watched his gazelle body languidly milling around the room. He had a hard-on in his gray boxer briefs. He asked if he could get in bed with me. I said yes, and then we kissed softly — so much more natural than the night before. Then he kissed down my body. Then he ate my pussy for infinity.

I went to space. I came on his tongue. I said, *Want to fuck a little?* and we fucked. I said, *Kill me with your arrow cock.* Then I gave him a very long, slow blow job until he got harder than he had been. He came in my mouth. I swallowed his cum.

We had until noon. We kissed, rubbed against each other. He talked to my pussy. He made out with it. We talked about concerts. That was disappointing. I didn't want to talk about anything cultural, anything tethered to society. I only wanted to talk about feelings, life in its most primal and essential form. There is something about the blankness of a hotel room that makes you feel like you can do that

— that such a thing as primal, essential life exists. There is something about occupying that neutral space with someone you really know nothing about — except the very essential, or the essential as they have painted it, or the essential as you have chosen to perceive it — that makes this seem possible.

When we said goodbye in the hotel lobby, I was aloof behind my sunglasses and under my fur hood (later he would text me a picture of himself in a jacket with a fur hood and sunglasses and say *look*). From behind my sunglasses and fur hood, I said, *We did good*. I said it like a pro, like a champ. I was very boys club, very *not attached*. I guess he liked that, because later he told me that he had to look at a Google map to figure out where he was going next, but he'd hid in a deli next door to the hotel to do it, because he didn't want to mess up the good ending.

lust (noun) — *intense eagerness or enthusiasm* (*The American Heritage Dictionary of the English Language*, fourth edition)

The second time was at the empty house of a friend in Brooklyn, two months later. I texted him all afternoon from the bathtub, soaking in oils. I said that it felt like a holiday. We texted back and forth screenshots of our favorite sexts from the past seven months, celebrating ourselves. I liked that he was traveling for hours by bus to see me. It felt romantic. I didn't think about the fact that I'd flown four thousand miles from Los Angeles to New York. I believed it was for work, and it sort of was — but if he wasn't going to be there I probably wouldn't have made the trip.

I remember when he arrived at the door in the night snow. I couldn't believe he was real again. Or maybe he was not fully real — not as I envisioned him — but his face and body and hair were real. I said, *Let me take off your fucking coat. I just want to take off your fucking coat.*

I remember walking up the stairs to the bedroom and asking if he had brought music. He said that he would eat my pussy to infinity again, this time while listening to Teen Daze. He licked me for an entire album. After it ended I came. I remember then having some kind of sex, maybe doggy style.

I was fascinated by his uncircumcised dick. He was my first uncircumcised one. I felt like a virgin again. I wanted his dick to be dirty so I could taste what was under his foreskin and really know him. But it was clean.

I remember being very hungry and going down into the kitchen with him to look for food. I remember eating an apple and talking to him about being alive. I don't remember what we decided being alive was or if we even attempted to make a consensus. Maybe we didn't even talk. He looked very alive. I felt it.

Here is what he later said of that time:

> I think about the ten or fifteen minutes we spent downstairs at your friend's, nudish, foraging for snacks, when you explained your tattoo in the living room, and I faced your bare shoulders and midriff, and long apple-eating arms, and I doubt you've ever looked more beautiful, or had better posture. When we went upstairs you switched to rap to do rougher sex. And I'd kissed you first thing through the door. And you periodically asked if I was nervous, and I reported with a number out of ten. And we fell asleep listening to mixes in the morning all entangled. And before that when I first awoke I told you about a dream, and I was actually very funny, and felt 100% me.

I remember getting on the subway together and asking him what street he grew up on in Somerville, Massachusetts. I had gone to college in that town, and we'd both been there at the same time when I was between eighteen and twenty-one and he was between nine and twelve. He said he grew up on Morrison Avenue. I had a therapist who lived on Morrison Ave. He laughed and said, *My mom is a therapist.* I asked for her name and when he told me, I said, *Oh god. Your mom was my therapist.* He said, *Oh god. We could have met. I remember being in her house that summer and seeing all the college girls going in and out and thinking they were hot.*

I got off the subway then and went to go meet up with my parents. I asked my mother if she remembered paying a large, unpaid therapy bill, when his mom had to call her, because I had not paid. She remembered. I think this is when I started feeling like something magic was going on. I cried in the bathroom.

love (noun) — strong affection for another arising out of kinship or personal ties (Merriam-Webster online dictionary)

infatuation (noun) — the first stage of a relationship before developing into a mature intimacy (Wikipedia)

I began sneaking hints to him about my real feelings. I wondered if he could actually see us being together. I would allude to this in roundabout ways, until finally, I texted him about it.

Me: sometimes i feel sad u r not mine. i feel sad that i am not younger, unmarried, living on the east coast, and i wonder if u ever feel that way. it is ok if u don't. and the way things are, the fantasy we have rendered is probably much better than that fantasy made real, but sometimes i want it a lot. this is a scary thing for me to txt u bc i don't want to txt u this and make u scared that i am "attachy" or "catching too many feels" and ruin what is a fun and beautiful thing, but i want to be true to myself and so i tell you the truth

Him: Thank you for this. Yes, I think of you this way. Meeting at a different place in time & space, being snuggling artbunnies together. I'm sad, in different ways. Like you said, there are advantages to what we have. This can potentially last indefinitely. We get to dodge the harder realities of daily compatibility and enjoy deep compatibility. If this is harder for you than me, I don't like that. I can't tell what extent u feel this but if u just wanted to say it I'm glad you did, and if there's more we should talk more. Is this what you meant by wanting to be a man, feels would be easier? You make me feel there's someone else in this empty high earth orbit. I feel very close to you when we have sex and share lifesadness and talk about the greater orbiting orbs. You're really good for me. I feel: the grass is sad everywhere, but at least we can kiss? I'm worried it's more double edged for you. I don't know how to be polyamorous. It's easy for my side. I feel a lot of pain at once, then feel kind of shocked and free. I don't know what it's like w other neurohormones. I want it to be okay for you. I want you to be my cosmos woman and I want to worship your mind & heartpussy always. I love you

To me this read like a love letter — some sort of affirmation, or that is how I wanted to see it. And of course, what I have not said up until now is that I was married. I was married to someone else — nonmonogamous at that time, but married — and so, perhaps, my own unavailability made it safe for me to imagine myself with this person and for him to play the game with me. The fantasy was inherently sustainable as a fantasy. It could stay a fantasy forever, if we wanted.

There was an odd, psychic quality to our relationship too. Every time we met I had my period. Somehow, he always knew that I would have my period. He said this was because he was in tune with what my pussy was doing. When he licked my pussy and got blood on his face, I thought he must really love me to lick my blood. But maybe that was more about him loving pussy — any pussy — than him loving me. Like, maybe there are just some men who love pussy so much that they will lick anyone's blood. Maybe it didn't matter that it was my blood. The sheets were always bloody.

One time, when we were apart, I wrote his name on a piece of paper in my menstrual blood and texted it to him. The paper is still in my journal and the blood is very faint brown-pink now. It looks prettier today than on the day I wrote it.

lust (noun) — a passionate or overmastering desire or craving (dictionary.com)

love (noun) — an intense emotional attachment (*The American Heritage Dictionary of the English Language*, fourth edition)

love (noun) — the emotion of sex and romance (*The American Heritage Dictionary of the English Language*, fourth edition)

Our final meeting lasted for an entire weekend. It was in a hotel all the way on the bottom tip of Manhattan. He texted me from the bus and I told him I would be taking a nap until he got there.

Sleep, sleep in my heroin, he said, meaning sleep in the anticipation. I said that I was having a stomachache and could he bring me some Pepto. I think it was the only thing he ever bought for me. I still have the Pepto tablets. To me, they still seem romantic: pink, cherry flavor. To me they look like tiny valentines.

That night I had my first anal sex. It was tender, nothing like I had seen in porn. I felt like we were a pair of twins sharing a womb, two DNA strands, two genderless humans. I felt that I was a virgin again. He ate my pussy as he always did, as it was our foundation of sorts. He licked my ass too. He put one finger in my ass, then two, then three. He really knew what to do. I really wanted it. We Frenched each other with his dick going in and out of my ass.

Afterward, I cried — not because it hurt but because of something else. I had the feeling that a darkness was lifting. I forgot about death.

The next day we went to go get lunch together and for the first time, we held each other's hands outside in public. I felt so proud to be holding his hand, not only because he was physically beautiful, but because he was keeping death away. We talked about bonobos, how they are nonmonogamous and use sex to pacify all kinds of situations. Verbally I agreed that more humans should be like bonobos. But inside, I thought, *I would be monogamous with you.*

Or maybe I did not let myself think that. Maybe I wanted him to be mine, but also wanted to continue to be married and also to fuck other men. I brought him to an event that night where I read poetry. Other men I had fucked were there. And the first time he had ever seen me, a year before, before the Internet flirtation and sexting began, it was at a poetry event like that. Both times I wore black. Both times there were other men I had fucked in the room.

On the cab ride back to the hotel, the driver put on "Stairway to Heaven". This would have been corny except that we were able to be corny together, as that is what children do together, and so it was not corny. We made out in the cab as the cab crossed over the Williamsburg Bridge. I cried in his mouth.

When we got back to the hotel we made love again. This time he came inside me. I said *I'm in love with you* or *I love you*. I don't remember which. He said it back. I don't remember which.

love (noun) — an assurance of affection (*Merriam-Webster* online dictionary)

love (noun) — unselfish, loyal, and benevolent concern for the good of another (*Merriam-Webster* online dictionary) *love (noun) — brotherly concern for others* (*Merriam-Webster* online dictionary)

I felt that we were moving past only fucking, into something else. Over text, I told him that sometimes the harshness of our sexts didn't fit how I felt anymore exactly. I asked if I could tell him the truth.

Me: when i say hardfucktalk, i'm talking about sexting i think. like, i really like it in the sheets sometimes (not like "skullfuck her till she is crying whore pig" totally degrading kind of stuff, but hot stuff). and i like it a lot in sexting too, as we do sometimes (i think we go hard sometimes and it's great) but i guess i just mean that like once in a while i wld type something in to txt you and then be like, oh shit, that's gonna sound too romantic, make it harder/make it funnier/ don't scare this kid.

Him: I don't think I'd ever be scared by something you'd send me. Send me real feelings when you want to. I want to receive them unconditionally… You're so beautiful I want to throw a land mine into a wall of cinder blocks and paint your lips with the dust cloud. Your face is like… So Hot… Bone structure… Eyes… Lips… And your body… Is… So, God… Shockingly good…

I want to kiss and lick you spiraling into a drainhole to be spat into the first human epoch in which the majority of things are good…

That was as far as he would meet me. It was a beautiful place to meet me, but it wasn't the impossible, which was what I needed. I wanted to see what was possible. I wanted to see if the impossible could somehow be possible. But when I asked for the impossible, the DNA dissolved. He became twenty-five again and I became — old. I became a woman again and he became a man again. I became the pursuer and he became the pursued, which for me was the worst of all.

Me: i feel… swept away by you… for a long time I have felt so hopeless… i don't know. a dark cloud.

Me: when i am with you I feel an extraordinary sense of hope. that's how i can best describe it. hope. like i have been in the dark for a long time and did not realize it until the light came on. but

Me: I guess what I am saying is that being with you has shown me there is something more beautiful than I could have imagined out there and I want the adventure of mad love and sexuality

Me: if i lived in new york wld u "date me"? :)

Him: Yeah I think so

Him: Yeah. Would I come see u and make love to you and talk about life and go to movies and museums and cool restaurants? Yeah

Him: But be careful in working me into your plans, bc I have no idea what lies for us outside the bounds of what we have now. Like, I don't know. But if more of what we've been doing is enough for you, I can give that to you & it's really good for me, too. I think that's what you're saying

I sat with this for a moment. I pretended that what he was saying was not what he was saying or that what he was saying was okay with me. I wanted it to be okay. I wanted to be cool.

Me: of course. i know from what you have said to me that you tend to chafe under the strain of a relationship… is what we have "real"? what is "real"? i don't know. what makes what we have beautiful is that it is, in a lot of ways, not of this world. i can feel your flesh but much else about it is imaginary.

Him: OK good, I wanted to say that. But what we have is real. I want to be for you what you are for me: a deep influx of love and energy, from the beyond place, absorbed above us, untouched by the earth. And it will help us live our worldly lives

Him: I want to give you joy and love from this place so you can use it where you need it. It's more powerful to use energy in a different realm from where you got it, like how pokemon level up way faster when they're traded jk

I was able to sit with the Pokémon. And then, a few days later, I could no longer sit with the Pokémon.

Me: hiii. so, i have been doing some thinking and some talking here in LA and have decided to give... monogamy a try. with my husband. but this means an end for you and me in a sexual/ sextual context. i am deeply sad as i write this. we did so good. good love. another lifetime? :)

Him: Okay. :) Obv bummed but way more important you do what's good in the long sense. Would be cool to reconnect on a literary basis in a while, but good to give it space

Me: who knows what is good? i am doing my best. i fell hard for you. you're that good. i wld have chosen you. and i wld have wanted you to be mine. but you belong to the world and the stars. i don't really know how to do things half-measures. i am sorry to do this over text. know that i'm crying at starbucks.

Me: and yes. space then literary/friendship even,
   sounds good.
Him: I'm wrenched. I'm not sure I can do things
   full measure, and for that I don't want sympathy,
   but I think you understand. I wish you all luck.
Me: Love to you. Goodbye for now
Him: Love to you. Goodbye.

We did try reconnecting a few months later, as friends. That lasted for about a month. I did a good job of pretending to be a wingman-type bro, all casual and chill. But inside I was suffering. I didn't want to just be friends. We would text about books, therapy, SSRIs, taking a shit at Walmart, but inside I was only wondering, *Does he still feel* _____*?* I guess he was too. Things devolved quickly into sexts about the Roman Empire and romantic emails. Then I said goodbye again. He got back in touch. Then I said goodbye for good.

What happens to the space that two people occupied together? How can it just disappear? Why can't it just become something else?

What I maybe miss most is being able to lapse into spaceland and fantasize about the sex with him. But it is no longer safe for me to do that. The fantasy is no longer safe. It is a death valley. Reality killed it. I also miss the many months of uncertainty of not knowing whether we could be. The nebulousness. Now I know we could not.

I want to text him and say: *hi*

I want him to text back: *Hi*

I want to say: *i am writing a personal essay about not knowing what love is. can i ask u some questions? were you in love with me or was it just the fucking? was i just an older woman who was so grateful just to be getting fucked by a younger man? (or other things I have read about older women fucking younger men on websites from the perspective of younger men?)*

I want to say: *was i real to you? could i have been real to you? why wasn't i?* I want to say: *when r u coming back to me in the way i want u?*

But he cannot answer me. My longing is not for him but for the stars. No, my longing is for him. Why is my version of him not real?

We got to be magic together. But is magic even real?

I want what is unreal to rescue me from the world. I want to be a shadow of myself dancing in a hotel room with his shadow. I want to be free.

I see him now in a dream and he has fallen for someone else. He comes to me in the dream and tells me he is about to be married. I ask him what I didn't have. Is it that I am old? Is my skin a crocodile? Was it that I am already married? Perhaps it is that I am of the stars and *he* is of the earth.

Who is the woman who has his whole being now? Does she have his whole being? Do I still live in there at all? I want to vomit up the whole thing and say, "But it was love."

When we think of our old lovers, and the people they are with now, we wonder what we did not have. We wonder collectively, as people, what other people have. A collective unconscious is formed, a cloud, and we laze around it and lie to each other. We tell each other we are better than one another, better than whoever he is with now. We tell it to each other, because we are well-meaning people. We tell it to each other in friendship.

Our single friends say they are going to be alone for the rest of their lives and we tell them they are crazy. We tell them they are definitely going to find someone. But how do we know? We know nothing.

It is our single friends who keep us in our marriages. They remind us that being single is sad. Dating is sad. Online dating is sad. Attending holidays and weddings alone is sad. Marriage, too, is sad.

But love, lust, infatuation — for a few moments, I was not sad.

Honk If There's a Committee in Your Head Trying to Kill You

The ocean gives me performance anxiety about being at peace. The moon is definitely judging me. Dogs know the truth. Babies see through me. Anything natural, anything pure: judging me.

People have said that I'm no better or worse than anyone else. I've been told that the universe probably wants me here. Still, I choose to feel that I am being judged as a piece of shit by some cosmic arbiter. The thing is, I'm self-centered. I guess I'd prefer some cosmic judge thinking shitty things about me, rather than nothing thinking about me at all. There are so many people and we're all awful in our own special ways; yet somehow, I'm the most profoundly, existentially awful. It seems unlikely that would be the case. But that's how I roll.

In an attempt to manipulate this elusive judge, one thing I like to do is play games that elevate superficial bullshit to the level of life and death. My favorite game is the one that I play with calories. Like, I pretend the cosmic arbiter is deeply concerned with my calorie intake. If the arbiter is judging me based on my calorie intake, then I can avoid judgment on a more profound level for worse shit. I can channel my more free-floating, all-consuming anxiety over the uncontrollable (i.e., the inevitability of death) into a much more manageable state of superficial, tangible anxiety. I can obsess about fruit and not my cosmic awfulness.

Thus, I know the caloric content of every single fruit and vegetable. A large apple is 100 calories. A large sweet potato is 165 calories. One thing I like to do is buy the biggest apples and sweet potatoes I can find (like human-head-size fruit, just really roided up and fucked) and still count them as 100 and 165 cals, respectively. Then I like to worry that I am getting fat off the misproportioned fruit. Then I like to ask people in a backwards way if I am getting fat by saying I am getting fat and hoping that they will negate me.

Sometimes the cosmic judge speaks through other people. Sometimes it speaks through my interpretations of how they perceive me (often totally imagined). More frequently, though, the judge speaks through a committee in my head. Right now the committee in my head is saying, *Why are you writing about your relationship to the calories in fruit, you privileged piece of shit? Nobody cares. There are bigger issues in the world.* What's sad is that I'm not even taking action on the bigger issues, because I'm too busy thinking about myself. But the committee says they're real.

The weird thing is that I also sometimes claim to believe that the judge has an opponent. The opponent to the judge is an equally powerful, loving force who always has my back. For the sake of efficiency I'll call this force *god*.

I claim to believe my god exists, because I have experienced its presence many times. I have experienced god through other human beings who have helped me. While individuals have let me down, collectively I've always been able to find help. My god is a horizontal god who works sideways on earth rather than vertically from heaven down.

Of course if I could choose my dream god it would be heroin. Like, that's the god I really want — a god who protects me completely from my own feelings and makes me feel blissed out 100% of the time. Except my god wouldn't be a false god, because I wouldn't be dependent on anyone or anything for it. And I would never come down. And believe me when I say that I have tried to make many tangible things into this god. And believe me when I say that you always come down.

When I first got sober off the big stuff — alcohol and drugs — not the twelve thousand other things I've become addicted to since then, I really wanted a god that I could put in my pocket, like a few pills of OxyContin or a flask, so that it would be close by when I needed it. The Jewish god I grew up with seemed kind of weird and punishing. I really liked the Buddha, because he seemed like he would make me cool. Everyone knows Buddhists are cool. Also, I liked purchasing statuettes of deities in New Age gift shops in the hope that they would "make me spiritual", and Buddha statuettes make a frequent appearance in these types of gift shops. But then I got hung up on whether my Buddha was the blue medicine Buddha or the Chinese laughing Buddha. So I started obsessing about that.

Then I got deep into the crystal game. I started carrying around special crystals that would ward off specific elements or feelings at various times. I started seeing the color violet everywhere and was like, *Must buy amethyst crystal now to reflect my spiritual vision*, but then another voice in my head was like, *Yo, this is getting expensive for a pile of rocks*. Every spiritual trinket I've purchased quickly loses its juju. In the temple it's magic, but at home it just becomes more crap.

Ultimately, I had to accept that god can't be purchased or harnessed in a particular object. I had to give even my conception of what god should look like to god. I had to surrender trying to conceive of what a higher power could be, with my limited human mind, to the great mystery itself. Otherwise, I was going to make myself crazier.

I still have to surrender my ideas about god on a daily basis. Just when I think I "have it", it changes. Like any relationship, my relationship with god keeps evolving the longer I stay in it.

The other day, a friend of mine who used to believe in god said she no longer believes and is now an atheist. She made atheism sound really good. I was feeling angry at god at the time and was like: *Fuck you, god, I don't believe in you either, you piece of shit.* But then I realized that not only was I still talking to a god I claimed not to believe in; I was talking to god as if god were some douchebro. And a douchebro god is kind of a human conception and probably not god. Let's face it, any kind of bro god is a human conception. If we can define god as a static entity using our human mind alone, it probably isn't that rad of a god.

This is not to say that if you conceive of your own god using your mind that it's an inherently shitty god. I think that we should all have our own gods, and whatever we believe exists does, in some way, exist. But, like, when I imagine god as a douchebro or as an asshole (which I've been conditioned to do as a result of being raised in the Jewish religion, where god is kind of a punishing dick), it's harder for me to find comfort in that god. I don't really want to go to it for help. Why would I?

God, for me, is more of a feeling, a feeling of peace. I think my god lives in a silence that exists inside me. It's such a delicious fucking silence, so profound. But this can also get tricky, because if I'm feeling crazy then I'm like, Where the hell is god? Has god abandoned me? Like, no peace, no god. But it's still better than some bro deity telling me I'm a piece of shit.

Also, the silence is always there. The silence doesn't go away. It's just that sometimes I don't hear or feel it, because the committee is so loud. The committee is a lot louder than the god-silence, and also it can seem more exciting. When the committee tells me about stuff I need to have, or am going to get, it's sexier than the silence of god. Also, the silence is just there, chillin', but the committee is working really hard to get my attention. When I'm sleeping, the committee stays up all night and then greets me at dawn with really bad ideas. It's like, *Good morning! Everything is shit! Time to act impulsively. But first let's start by getting into fights with imaginary people from the past. Next let's catalog everything that's wrong with you and your life. Also, I want to remind you of everything you don't have — and everything you should be scared of losing. Let's begin.*

Sometimes I try to placate the committee by doing what it tells me. I shop or eat or send emails I shouldn't be sending. I chase attention. I watch too much porn. But ultimately, I can't escape the committee by feeding it anything external or trying to run away from myself. There will never be enough stuff to sate the committee. It only gets hungrier and runs faster.

The only chance I have to find respite from the committee, even just for a few minutes, is to get totally still. If I get really still and quiet, sometimes the committee will talk and talk until it has nothing left to say and then it finally shuts the fuck up. It seems counterintuitive to hang out with the assholes in my head who are trying to kill me, so as to defeat them. But this is what I have found to be effective. This is why I have to meditate every morning.

My morning meditation practice is nothing intense. It's ten minutes, first thing, before I go on the Internet (the committee loves the Internet!). Sometimes I do a mantra or wish loving-kindness upon four people: myself, a loved one, a stranger, and a person I dislike at the moment. Mostly, though, it's just me staying still long enough to get to the silence under the committee. If I am really still, I get to ask the silence questions and it gives me good answers.

The silence is always there, under the committee. But I usually have to spend the first eight minutes of my meditation getting yelled at by the committee before I get to the silence. Like, mostly I am meditating on how fucked I am.

A typical meditation is: *Hare Krishna (you're an oversharing loser) Hare Krishna (you totally come off as needy) Krishna Krishna (stop texting people back so quickly) Hare Hare (don't initiate texts either) Hare Rama (your tits are sagging) Hare Rama (your nipples were never that good) Rama Rama (it's basically over) Hare Hare (you're basically dead).*

Right before the end of the meditation, the committee stops. It's not gone for good, but it shuts up for a second. That's when I get the moment of peace I've been searching for my entire life. It's what alcohol and drugs did so beautifully for me at first, before I came down. If I could have stayed drunk all the time, I wouldn't have had to get sober. But I couldn't, so I did.

I don't think my meditation practice inherently makes me spiritual. I haven't ascended and I'm not enlightened. I'm no better than anyone else (if anything, I just require more help). But what the practice gives me is a chance of staying on the planet. When I meditate, I go from being a 96% impulsive and self-obsessed person to a 92% impulsive and self-obsessed person. That 4% keeps me alive.

It's like every morning I access this template for pause in my brain. Then, as I go about my day and the voices start up again, I have a frame of reference that these voices might not be the whole truth. They may feel completely true, but there is also a memory of quiet beneath them, which shows that they maybe aren't giving me the full picture of reality. They might be lying about me being a total piece of shit.

But who really wants to sit quietly and be still with the voices? I certainly don't. Sometimes I'll go without meditation for a few days, because I'm having a really good time running my life on self-will and I don't want god, silence, or the space for reflection to piss on my party. Like, I don't want to see what I'm doing. I don't want to see that I'm about to make a mess. The committee is like: *You're killin' it! Don't stop!* But inevitably, I always crash and return to my meditation practice again.

There is a large part of me, the committee, that wants to see me dead. If it can't kill me, it'll settle for seeing me miserable. It wants me spinning out on what I lack, talking to myself. I don't know why these forces exist in me that want me to die, I guess I'm just wired that way. But it's cool that there is this other part of me that must really want to live. I don't have scientific proof of its existence, and I don't need it. I'm still alive. So I know it's there.

I Took the Internet Addiction Quiz and I Won

How are my feelings not going to kill me? The Internet is going to save me from my feelings. But what is going to save me from the Internet? I am dopamine's girl. I am a puppy for attention from imaginary people. I am lonely among real human beings and would rather be on my phone than engage with reality.

The Internet has given me the dopamine, attention, amplification, connection, and escape I seek. It has also distracted me, disappointed me, paralyzed me, and catalyzed a false sense of self. The Internet has enhanced my taste for isolation. It has increased my solipsism and made me even more incapable of coping with reality.

Reality was never my first choice.

I like that I can be somebody else on the Internet. I like that I can present one facet of myself and embody that. I don't have to live in a body on the Internet. It's so much easier to present an illusion of oneself than to contain multitudes. Illusion is easier than flesh. I like that other people can be a hologram version of themselves on the Internet, too. I like tweets and nudes, romantic emails, avatars and dick pics. I like that I get to fill in the blanks. Who are you? I'll decide.

I've long thought that the word *illusion* meant a better version of reality. But recently, after being forced to mourn a series of illusions — most of them romantic, each of them Internet in origin — I looked up the word *illusion* in the dictionary. I was surprised to discover that the word *illusion* actually means "something that deceives by producing a false or misleading impression of reality". So, an illusion is not inherently a better version of reality. An illusion is a false version of reality. An illusion is a lie.

This discovery has changed the nature of my relationship with illusion. I feel like I am mourning the death of a whole way of seeing the world. I see more clearly now. I see myself trying to patch a hole inside me that cannot be patched by anything external. I am cobbling together the dregs of what I can still use to get high into a shitty dopamine party. That party is the Internet.

But is my obsession with the Internet actually an addiction? I've decided to answer that question by taking a quiz from Psych Central called "Are You Addicted to the Internet?" While the quiz is multiple choice, my relationship with the Internet is complex, and so I have chosen to write my responses in essay form.

1. How often do you find that you stay online longer than you intended?

I like to use my iPhone in bathrooms. I've spent hours on the toilet not peeing. Sometimes it's my own toilet. Sometimes I'm out in the world and I excuse myself to use the bathroom. I always tell myself five minutes. It's never five minutes. I fall down a hole and the vanishing feels good. People think I'm dead. I like it.

I try to set rules around my Internet usage. The act of rule-setting means that I am probably an Internet addict. Like, people who aren't addicts don't need to set rules about things. They just do them.

Some of my rules include: 10 minutes of meditation before turning on phone or computer in the morning, no social media before noon, only 120 minutes on social media websites per day, only two tweets per day and only after seven p.m., Internet detox for twenty-four hours on weekend. I break them all daily.

2. Do you prefer the excitement of the Internet to intimacy with your partner?

Yes. Of course. Unless the partner is a virtual stranger

upon whom I have projected a fantasy narrative and we are making out for the first time in a hotel room.

3. Do you neglect household chores to spend more time online?

When something real has to be done, like making the bed or paying a bill, I feel like it is going to kill me. Like, I feel that a cruel and oppressive mother is coming for me and the world is comprised of nothing but Sisyphean tasks, wherein you infinitely push a boulder up a hill and are infinitely crushed. One time I was hand washing underwear in the sink and then I got on Twitter and the sink overflowed and the neighbor downstairs, who just had a baby, sent the building manager up and the building manager busted in and I thought he was a serial killer. So, yes.

4. Does your work (or school work) suffer because of the amount of time you spend online?

My work is online.

5. Do you form new relationships with others online?

I would rather be on the Internet engaging with half-imaginary people in a fake way than in real life engaging with real people in a real way. Not that everything on the Internet is fake. I have forged some deep connections with people I've never met (or maybe I was connecting with myself — my own desire for who I wanted them to be) via the Internet. Sometimes I compare the IRL people in my life with the Internet people in my life and I always feel like, Why can't the IRL people be more like the Internet people? This is maybe because real people aren't pixelated. Their mistakes and annoyingness can't be repurposed into a fantasy. I actually have to see the real people and be seen by them. If people never become real, it's harder for them to disappoint you. That's why the Internet is good for sad people. You can be with people without having to be with people.

6. Do others in your life complain to you about the amount of time you spend online?

It's going to be the death of my main relationship. The person with whom I am in a primary relationship calls my phone my "boyfriend". He becomes elated when the battery dies. One time he threatened to throw it out the window. He is way more concerned with the way I use the Internet to shut him out than anything I could do sexually with another person. I tell him that I am not shutting him out. I am shutting out reality. Unfortunately for him, he is real.

7. Do you become defensive or secretive when anyone asks you what you do online?

It's more about the act of being online, itself, than what I am doing there. Everyone knows what I am doing there. I'm tweeting. It's more about the bathroom thing. I will say to the person with whom I have a relationship "I have to poop." And then I'm gone for the rest of the night.

Actually, one thing I am ashamed of is that I like "female friendly" porn. Like, I wish that I didn't like "female friendly" porn. I wish that when I watched Xander Corvus eat "babysitter" Melanie Rios's pussy, I wasn't like, *Omg he is so in love with her. Like, he has def been in love with her the whole time she has been his babysitter and he has dreamt of this moment and now it is here and he will def want to be with her forever.* I wish I wasn't like that.

8. Have you ever noticed that your job performance or productivity suffers because of the time spent online?

Obvi.

9. Do you check your email before something else that you need to do?

I can't even get involved in email anymore, because it usually requires more than 140 characters. If I do send an email, I use Siri to do it and dictate the thing.

So, the Internet has destroyed my attention span to the extent that I can no longer email. The Internet has gotten me off of email. The iPhone has gotten me off the laptop. If the laptop is cocaine, the iPhone is crack. And I take these hits of crack before, during, and after everything.

10. Do you snap, yell, or act annoyed if someone bothers you while you are online?

I'm usually in a comatose state and not aware of the world around me. When I'm down the rabbit hole, I don't see you.

11. Do you find yourself anxiously anticipating when you will go online again?

I've had the shakes.

12. Do you block out disturbing thoughts about your life with soothing thoughts of the Internet?

My biggest fear is dying. Death is fine, but dying itself — the inability to breathe, the final panic attack — is really scary. I'm also scared of life itself, since dying is implicit in life. Sometimes life seems hyperreal. Like, I look at people and they look like robots or like they are made of rubber and I think I am witnessing the lifting of a matrix, but it's probably just anxiety. In those moments I am like,

Damn, no one knows what's really going on here. My therapist doesn't help. She can't explain what's going on here any better than anyone else. She can't stop me from dying. The Internet can't either, but it's a good place to tether that adrenaline. It's easier than rubber people.

Another thing I am afraid of is rejection. If anyone is going to reject me, I'd rather it be me. When a real human being rejects my IRL self, or I perceive a rejection of my IRL self, I need confirmation that I am worthy of being on the planet. The way that I achieve this confirmation is to garner fake love from strangers via an avatar that resembles me.

These attempts at reparation of my core self, or lack of core self, always result in a cascade of binge tweeting. I immediately follow the binge by deleting all or most of the tweets and then follow the mass deletion with a shame spiral.

13. Do you fear that life without the Internet would be boring, empty, or joyless?

No, I think it would be beautiful. I imagine myself on a rocky beach, clutching something green. It's probably seaweed, but maybe it's moss. I drink a lot of chamomile tea. I "show up" for myself. Yeah, it would be empty.

14. Do you find yourself saying "just a few more minutes" when online?

If there is anything I don't like, it's linear time. The Internet makes me feel like I can bend time. I can't bend time, so I just say "five more minutes" and then fall into a vortex. I go into blackouts.

15. Do you feel preoccupied with the Internet when off-line, or fantasize about being online?

Obvi.

16. Do you lose sleep due to being online late at night?

This morning I woke up at three a.m. and went online. It's now six thirty in the morning. I've done that every night this week, except for Monday, when I didn't go to sleep at all. I think the Internet replicates the sun. Maybe goth/emo/highly sensitive people shouldn't be on the Internet. We are bound to wither.

17. Do you try to hide how long you've been online?

When I was still drinking, I used to show up at bars, already drunk, and quickly order a drink. I'd pretend that first drink at the bar had gotten me drunk. I kept my So Sad Today Twitter account anonymous, partly because I was embarrassed by how much I tweet. I feel like there is a connection here.

18. Do you choose to spend more time online over going out with others?

The Internet means I get to be with people without leaving the house. Also, I can be anybody I want to be. Like I can be a fucking wizard on the Internet while, in reality, I am here eating Weight Watchers lasagna and wearing a pair of boxer shorts with trumpets on them.

19. Have you tried to cut down the amount of time you spend online and failed?

Every day.

20. Do you feel depressed, moody, or nervous when you are off-line, which goes away once you are back online?

Actually, a lot of times I go on the Internet and it's the Internet that makes me depressed, moody, and nervous. Like, I go on there and two seconds later I'm like, *fuck everything*. But IRL is somehow still worse.

There is something about the Internet that, even when it sucks, holds infinite potential at all times. Like, I may know a site is going to suck, because it just sucked a second ago, but I keep hitting refresh. Eventually it changes. But life isn't like that. When I keep hitting refresh on the same thing in life I keep getting the same thing. Making the same mistakes + expecting different results = fuck.

Actually, maybe that's not entirely true. There's a spirituality in repetitive things: malas, mantras, rosaries, Hail Marys, or as Prince said, *joy in repetition*. The problem with addiction is that the joy in repetition eventually gives way to a combination of both joy and problems. Then it gives way to just problems.

I think that the Internet's grasp on me has something to do with its light and blankness. The light and blankness are sexy and they make me feel like anything is possible. I am sure that life holds the same infinite potential that the Internet holds. But unfortunately, I'm forced to be a grown-up in life. On the Internet I'm still sixteen.

Also, I've done well at the Internet. If Twitter is a video game, I've beaten it. I haven't always done well at life. I haven't beaten the fact that I am going to die one day. The cheat code for dying is what?

I just don't see myself ever walking a middle path with the Internet. It's probably going to have to be all or nothing. Like, harm reduction never worked for me. Once a cucumber turns into a pickle, you can't turn it back into a cucumber. And I've been pickled by the Internet for a long time.

I Don't Feel Bad About My Neck

I don't feel bad about my neck. My neck is okay. It's holding its own. It doesn't look old yet.

I feel bad for using the word *old* as synonymous with *bad*. Where did I learn that to look old as a woman is bad? Maybe I learned it, like, everywhere.

I feel bad that I was more upset when this dude told people I look old, than when I found out he was an alleged rapist. I didn't even confront him about the rape allegations. I just said, *Thanks for telling people I look old. That was really fucking great to hear.*

I feel bad about my knees. I have MILF-y knees and I don't even have children. I'm a childless MILF with old knees.

I feel bad for judging people who have children. Recently I was at the Cheesecake Factory (which is one of my favorite restaurants and I feel bad about that) and I saw this very Cheesecake Factory–looking couple with their baby. I thought, *Oh great, just what we need, another American.* They looked happy. I felt like they were wrong.

I feel bad about my deeper, underlying reasons

for judging people with children. I judge them as a defense mechanism, because I am sad about my motivations for not having kids. I am self-centered and dysmorphic with low self-esteem. I am scared I would give birth to my own childhood self-hatred. I am scared I would give birth with my head in the oven.

I feel bad that I don't identify with the purity of babies. I used to think I would just adopt an older child one day — that way I wouldn't have to do the initial fucking it up. But now I think the only thing I am equipped to deal with less than my own child is someone else's child.

I feel bad that when I interact with children I assume they are judging me.

I feel bad that sometimes I wish to just be struck pregnant. I don't want to make the decision to get pregnant. If I actively choose to have a child, then the child can look at me and say, "I never asked to be born." But if I get knocked up, then I can just blame it on "the universe". This is disempowering, irresponsible, and ignores the reality of abortion. Yet I find it comforting.

I feel bad about my vagina. The right inner labia is longer than the left inner labia. I swear I can trace this to the time my high school boyfriend fingered me really hard in the car and I wasn't wet. It hurt, but I didn't tell him to stop or lick it first, because I didn't think it mattered that it hurt. I remember the dry right labia getting sort of "caught" in the friction of the fingering. When I went home that night, the right labia looked like a blowfish. It never really unswelled.

I feel bad that my vagina used to be more pink. As I remember, it was totally pink. Now the inner labia have turned more purple with age. Now, when someone refers to it as my *tight pink pussy* I feel like they're lying.

I feel bad that I wax off all my pubes. What kind of artist waxes off all of her pubes? I should at least leave a stripe or triangle on top, and just wax my asshole, inner thighs, and outer labia if I'm going to wax at all. But my problem with leaving the triangle, or a strip, is that during the grow-out phase, my OCD really flares up. Like, if there are two lengths of pubic hair "on the mound" it makes me anxious. I feel like it looks mullet-y.

I feel bad that my pubic hair isn't aligned with the current pubic hair trend among porn stars, which is all-bare plus triangle on top. I feel bad that my pubic hair isn't aligned with the current pubic hair trend among hippie girls, either. My friend who lives in Maine with a bunch of hip, organic homesteader women said that the girls in Maine are waxing. But they leave a big triangle on top to give the illusion of not waxing. To me, these girls are cheating. If you are going to get that organic farm-girl cred, then you should probably earn it by not waxing your pussy at all. Far be it from me to tell another woman what she should do with her pussy. But it just seems a little unfair. They get homesteader cred and a clean butthole? No.

I feel bad that I'm afraid to not wax my pubic hair at all — to just leave that shit alone — because I am afraid of rejection. Like, I'm afraid that if I let it grow in, it will be too painful to ever wax off again (the first time I ever got waxed, I lay on the table with half a lip waxed off and the other one hairy, crying *I'm a feminist*). I'm afraid that I will have sex with someone who prefers no pubes and sees me as less-than, because I have a big, hairy bush. True, I could have sex with someone who loves pubes and feel judged about my bare pussy. But, like, the other way feels scarier.

I feel bad that when I see feminism used as clickbait, it kind of makes me want to puke or die. This is not a condemnation of the contemporary feminist movement (or movements), but a revulsion to clickbait. To engage in depth with the ephemeral that is marketing culture makes my inner witch nauseous. I feel like if I read the article I am being poisoned. Like, I am a vampire and clickbait is my garlic, and to turn feminism into clickbait is just a giant fucking puke — and not the sexy kind.

I feel bad that I see myself more as a witch than any kind of -ist. I have a tendency to shrink from -ists. It might be because I am an isolator and have social anxiety, and don't like groups or labels. Having said that, feminism is implicit in my witchery.

I feel bad that I don't know what makes me a witch, I just know that I am one.

I feel bad that I am a crappy witch when it comes to my body. Like, what the fuck kind of witch eats Lean Cuisine mac and cheese and not Kraft full-fat macaroni and cheese, or regular homemade mac and cheese (or vegan mac and cheese, if she is a steward of the earth and all of god's creation, which seems to me would be implicit in being the best witch and best feminist/humanist/person one could be). If I were the CEO of a coven I would be like, "Yo, this Lean Cuisine–eating witch is unacceptable." Though, if I were truly the ultimate witch I would accept where I am and embrace me, so maybe in that way if I were the ultimate feminist I would do the same. But there is still no embrace. I just cannot seem to give myself that hug of the divine mother that is like, *baby baby baby it's okay.*

I feel bad that I don't have a dick. I tend to think

that some of my struggles with living in a body are because it is a female body. I tend to think that if I had a male body then all of my problems would be solved, but that's probably false. If I had a dick I'd probably never get it up.

I feel bad that even though I want a dick, it's a casual want. For the most part, I identify with my physical gender. I feel bad that I can live without the fear of intimidation, harassment, or getting the shit kicked out of me for wanting to be what I am, whereas transgender people still can't.

I feel bad that when it comes to dicks I've been a size queen in the past. I think my desire for a man with a big dick has to do with the fact that the dick I'm fucking always feels like it's my own. It's my surrogate dick. Like, if I have a dick, I want it to be big. But truthfully, big dicks and medium dicks feel the same inside.

I feel bad that when a younger person tried to suck my tits recently, there were depth-perception issues involving sagging. Like, I think he expected the nipple to be higher up than it was. The first time he went for the nipple he missed. I feel bad that when I wrote a poem about the incident he thought that I was accusing him of being in love with his mother. What the poem was actually attempting to say was that I hoped he was in love with his mother, because if he could be in love with his mother, then maybe he could forgive my droopiness. Maybe it would even turn him on extra. That poem sucked.

I feel bad that when the younger person told me my pussy tasted like *rain and a mountain spring and a Fabergé egg and a waterfall cave where celebs meditate*, I felt proud. I feel bad for feeling proud. Why is a waterpussy better than a bitterpussy or a salmonpussy? Also, I don't think my pussy always tastes that pure. I washed hard for him. I washed every time.

I feel bad that the younger person has stopped faving my tweets and didn't "like" my Facebook post about going to a police brutality protest.

I feel bad that I posted about the police brutality protest on Facebook in the first place. By posting about the police brutality protest, I thought I was spreading the word — but now I feel like I was commodifying something that is not mine, as a white woman, to commodify. I don't want to appropriate anyone's pain.

I feel bad that I got kind of high on the vibes at the police brutality protest. Like, I cried and it felt cathartic, and it's a catharsis that was not mine to have. Since I'm a white girl, the cops have never fucked with me. Is there a difference between being supportive of other people's revolutions vs. turning something tragic into your own experience? I think there is.

I feel bad that I brought a Prada bag to a police brutality protest.

I feel bad that as a white girl I can go shopping in certain stores and won't be eyed, bothered, humiliated, kicked out, unlawfully arrested, or shot, and that the same is true for me of pretty much all places, institutions, and public parks. That's not true for all human beings.

I feel bad about my struggle, because it is nothing compared to other people's struggles and yet it still hurts.

I feel bad about this essay.

I feel bad about this book.

The Patron Saint of
Nicotine Gum

Here's why I'm afraid of life after death: What if there is no nicotine gum?

I must have access to my nicotine gum at all times. I kiss with the gum. I sleep with the gum. Anything you can do without the gum I must do with the gum. I am chewing the gum right now.

I chew the gum, because I don't trust the universe to fill me up on its own. I can't count on the universe to sate my many holes: physical, emotional, spiritual. So I take matters into my own hands. I give myself little "doggy treats" for being alive. Each time I unwrap a new piece of nicotine gum and put it in my mouth (roughly every thirty minutes), I generate a sense of synthetic hope and potentiality. I am self-soothing. I am "being my own mommy". I am saying, *Here you go, my darling. I know life hurts. I know reality is itchy. But open your mouth. A fresh chance at happiness has arrived!*

I've been chewing nicotine gum for twelve years. I haven't had a cigarette in ten years. So you might say the gum works, except now I have a gum problem. I am so addicted to the gum that I have to order it from special "dealers" in bulk on eBay. I get gum on all the bedding. There are many reasons why I don't think I will have children, but the necessity of getting off the gum during pregnancy is one of them. When it comes down to anything vs. the gum, I always choose the gum.

Now let me just say, before we go any further, that if you're thinking of using nicotine gum to quit smoking you should not let my experience scare you. I am the addict's addict. Everything I touch turns to dopamine. I can even turn people into dopamine (ask me how!).

My first cigarette was a Marlboro Red that I stole from my dad and smoked alone in front of my bedroom mirror. I felt a sudden coldness in my lungs, exhaled sexily, and then the room spun around. The vertigo scared me, as do all abrupt shifts in consciousness (I prefer a steady high). I was fourteen.

My next cigarettes, at sixteen, were Marlboro Lights that I shared with a boyfriend under the stars. They were make-out cigarettes — cigarettes of romance, possibility, and freedom. I noticed that when I smoked I became less hungry, which I loved, because I really wanted to be skinny.

Cigarettes soon became meal postponers, or — when paired with Diet Coke and Trident cinnamon gum — meal replacements. I quickly became a pack-a-day smoker, often two, and required a cigarette smoked out my bedroom window just to leave the house in the morning. I smoked outside the gym. I smoked on Rollerblades. I smoked Marlboro Lights and Parliaments, vanilla bidis and cloves. During a Jim Morrison phase I smoked American Spirits.

My mom didn't smell my cigarettes because of my dad's smoking. She believed that my dad had quit, even though the car was full of ash, the garage was full of butts, and she saw him smoking through the window every night. My mom would watch my dad smoke and say, *No, he doesn't smoke*. So the smell of cigarettes somehow equated a nonsmoker. So I was left alone.

I then went to college and the logistics of my smoking became an issue. I had a roommate who claimed to be a smoker, but she was a "social smoker" and I was a "never-not-smoking smoker". When she saw and smelled the level of my compulsion she issued a moratorium on smoking in our room. The room then became an unsafe place for me, as was any place where I couldn't smoke.

Thus commenced a cycle of smoking regulations by other roommates and friends. I preferred to chain-smoke in isolation rather than not smoke among others. I only felt comfortable around people who smoked like me (every moment, back-to-back, like breathing). Cigarettes had become a problem, and the problem was: How could I consume enough of them while living in society?

I bought my first box of Nicorette at age twenty before a flight to London. I knew that I couldn't get through the seven hours without some hits of nicotine, and I don't like suffering. On the flight, a glorious new chapter in the annals of my addictions was revealed to me. I discovered that I wasn't fiending. The gum even gave me a secret buzz. The best part was, nobody knew I was "smoking" except me. I had arrived.

For the next few years I both smoked and chewed the gum. Sometimes I alternated between the two and sometimes I did a simultaneous smoke 'n chew. Then, over time, the gum's anytime-anywhere qualities won my heart. Nothing enhances addiction like access and secrecy, and the gum trumps cigarettes in both.

Imagine you have a special friend you can take with you into any situation. This friend makes you comfortable in your own skin. She helps you not need other people so much. The friend protects you from life and nobody has to know but you. Just put the friend in your mouth.

The way you chew nicotine gum is not to actually

chew it. When you first pop a piece of nicotine gum, you give it one to two quick chomps with your teeth and then park it, so the nicotine can seep in through your gums or tongue. I'm a left-side cheek parker, and my proclivity to stick to one side has led to some health scares.

There was a period when the whole left side of my tongue and cheek turned bright white. I was sure I had oral cancer, but the dentist said it was irritation from the intense flavor of the gum. I began rotating mouth sides and made the sad transition away from more intense flavors, like "coated fruit chill", "coated cinnamon", and "coated mint" Nicorette, into the gentler realm of Habitrol. Habitrol possesses a creamier quality — like a marshmallow vs. a candy cane. At no time did I say, "I'm giving up the gum."

I've also spoken with some physicians about the gum. They said that chewing the gum is better than smoking, but the constant nicotine is probably bad for my heart. But I feel like I have two hearts, a physical heart and an emotional one. And while the gum may have an adverse effect on my physical heart, it does wonders for my emotional one. It ballasts and buffers, nurtures and excites. I guess I value my emotional heart more.

I do recognize that my dependence on the gum reflects an inability to be still with myself, to be alone in the present moment. Also, I feel that the gum creates a barrier to intimacy between me and other people. It's never just me and another person, it's me, another person, and the gum. But the present moment is scary. And intimacy can be terrifying. So the dilution of my beingness, or dare I say, aliveness, is a sacrifice I am willing to make to have an ally in this world: something that gives me a feeling of control, excitement, meaning, structure.

Like, I just want to be okay in this world. I don't trust myself to find that okayness alone. I guess I don't really trust the universe to give it to me, either. I want to know exactly where my next peace of mind is coming from. And it feels good to know that something has my back, even if it makes my life really small and might kill me.

My Vomit Fetish, Myself

One way to feel isolated is to unintentionally develop an odd sexual fetish at a very young age. Next, spend your adolescence reinforcing that fetish through masturbation, until you can only reach orgasm in relation to that very specific fantasy. After that, live your teen years in fear of revealing your secret sexual preference. Eventually, you might want to let a few sexual partners know of your fetish, but definitely downplay it. Never invite any sexual partners to render your fantasies real, or to engage your inner world through role-play, thereby cordoning off a very important piece of you from ever knowing true sexual intimacy for the remainder of your life. Trust me, it works.

My fetish is vomit. Not vomit itself, but the act of vomiting. Vomiting is hot. It's a primal, involuntary act — much like ejaculation. There's guttural sounds and animalistic faces. It's gross but it's real.

I don't like vomiting much, myself. But I want to watch people vomiting. Or I want to be a person who is not me vomiting. Mostly I want to do this in my head.

I think my vomit fetish started when I threw up in my sleep at three years old. My mother, who wasn't the traditional nurturing type, behaved in a way that was very nurturing toward me. She cuddled me and gently bathed me. My own powerlessness, coupled with a new experience of tender care — her acceptance of me at my most disgusting — was intoxicating. Now, not only did I know that my mother really loved me, but she loved me at my most vile. When you have low self-esteem, to be embraced at your most vile is a marvel.

I had my first orgasm at age ten, humping a four-foot George Jetson doll while a homemade tape of vomiting sounds (my own, fake) played on my Walkman. I fantasized that I was Kimberly, a pretty, popular gymnast-girl. I imagined that I/Kimberly was running down the hallway at my school, not making it to the bathroom, vomiting all over the place in front of everyone. I wanted this pretty girl to know shame, the shame that I felt in my own body. This turned me on. At the same time, I felt that Kimberly — as a pretty and popular girl — was beyond reproach. Even when out of control, even at her most disgusting, she would be embraced. I wanted to experience that as well.

In retrospect, I may have simply been sexually attracted to Kimberly, vomit or no vomit. But it was easier to mask this attraction with a vomit narrative than to grapple with the terrifying thought that I might be into girls.

So I humped George Jetson and imagined that I was Kimberly vomiting. I also imagined that I was a girl helping Kimberly vomit. As I humped I felt better and better. Then, a miracle occurred. From my vagina to my legs, I was suddenly rocketed beyond the space-time continuum. For a few moments, I was taken completely out of my own ego into a soul world of pleasure. I couldn't believe that this feeling existed. It seemed crazy that I had never heard about this before! Had I invented it? I patched up George (his stuffing was falling out) and joined my family downstairs for dinner. But I knew what I would be doing later. I was going to give myself this feeling forever.

Kimberly is still a lurking fantasy for me. I am very loyal to my fantasies, and once I get a good one I hold on to it for life. Here are a few of my other favorite vomit fantasies:

• I am having sex with a hot Roman emperor. We have just feasted. The Roman emperor is fucking me and vomiting at the same time.

Sometimes in this fantasy, I, myself, am the Roman emperor. Or I am watching.

• I am an obese, very femme woman on a business trip. I binge eat in a hotel room. One of the things I binge eat is a bad tuna sandwich. Then I go to an office to deliver a PowerPoint presentation. In the midst of the presentation I show visible signs of nausea. I escape to the bathroom and begin dry heaving. A powerful butch lesbian follows me to the bathroom and asks to be let in. At first I am resistant, because I feel ashamed. But then I let her in. The butch woman is deeply attracted to me: my body, my mind, and my vomiting. Other employees can hear me vomiting and they can hear her helping me vomit. When I am slightly recovered, she takes me home to her house, where she goes down on me for, like, three hours. I think we get married.

• I am a Chinese prince of the Ming dynasty. I am receiving a blow job and being caressed by multiple concubines. While I am getting the blow job I begin to vomit. One of the concubines gets excited and accepts the vomit into her mouth with great delight. The other concubines continue to blow and caress me as I vomit into her mouth.

• I am a six-foot-tall frat bro: hung and cut. I am the alpha of the pack, the broest of bros. I do a series of beer bongs in the frat house. Then I begin burping loudly. A fellow frat bro, who is secretly gay but not out, hears me burping and gets turned on. He then stands behind me as I vomit and rubs my back and abs. He wants me.

These are all fairly loving fantasies. What unites them, aside from vomit, is that each of them involves a complete acceptance and embrace. While some of them delight in the shaming of someone beautiful and/or powerful, the ultimate resolution of that shame is always self-acceptance by way of another's acceptance. To me, that's sexual fulfillment.

When searching for emetophilic porn (an emetophile is the name for a person with a vomit fetish) on sites like pornhub, you'll mostly find women gagging and vomiting on dicks. This doesn't do it for me. In those videos, the power is going in the wrong direction. It's too forced. I like a natural vomit. I like a vomit that comes as a surprise to the vomiter. But the Internet has served to enhance my vomit fetish fantasies. I've just had to google a lot.

Ten years ago I found a wonderful website called Slaveboy's Vomit Fetish, which featured videos, audio, images, and even erotic fiction (my favorite) of people vomiting. When I first discovered the website I felt like I had unearthed a treasure trove. I was excited that there were people like me out there and I couldn't believe how openly they talked about their fetish on the chatboard — even when they did so anonymously. Sadly, Slaveboy's is now defunct. I wish I had saved some of the stories in a Word doc.

Since then, I've found vomitonline.com (also now defunct; it's a fairly niche fetish) and vomitinbrazil.com (a paid site, but they used to have good previews), and I've also downloaded my fair share of pirated content.

Mostly I've scoured YouTube and collected tons of awesome videos of vomiting people. I have my favorites, usually videos that involve a lot of burping. Burping, to me, is the most sexual element of vomiting, because the sound is so primal. In my fantasies, the vomiters always burp a lot. I frequent the burp fetish forums, though I never leave a comment. One girl on the forums says her ultimate fantasy is a guy burping into her vagina as he gives her head. I'd have to agree that's a sexual ideal.

If you've masturbated to porn, or just masturbated in general, you know that feeling of shame you sometimes feel immediately following orgasm. Sometimes you look at the scene on the screen — or the scene that was just playing in your mind — and feel like, *What? I got off to this?* Now imagine that scene involves copious vomit.

I don't know if it's that shame that has led me to never incorporate vomiting into my actual sex life. There is a big difference between what goes on inside my head and the tactile experience of that attempted fantasy. I don't even know if I like vomit in real life. Whenever a person around me is vomiting, I get kind of scared and avoidant. This is called emetophobia.

I've never been the "let me hold your hair" type. Instead I run away. This resistance to IRL vomiting is likely a defense mechanism I've built up over time so that no one finds out my secret. Like, I don't want to appear too interested in vomiting people.

Most of my lovers haven't known of my fetish. With my first lover, I faked all of my orgasms. With subsequent lovers, I've often secretly employed a vomit fantasy while he or she was going down on me, so as to be able to achieve orgasm. I've heard from more than one lover that one minute I'm present and then I am suddenly totally detached during sex. I just "drift off". I think I know the reason why.

I've tried to privately "train myself" away from vomit over the years. I've masturbated to more vanilla fantasies so that I might better achieve orgasm with a partner without having to drift off. Some of my masturbation fantasies no longer involve vomit, but they always take longer. And when I'm with a partner, the fantasy is usually a requirement in order to climax. Vomit is my safe space.

I have told a few long-term partners about my fetish. These moments of bravery are usually then followed by years of backpedaling. When I come clean, I always end up eventually downplaying the fetish because of residual shame. The worst is when I'm watching a movie with a partner who knows of my fetish and somebody vomits on-screen. In those moments, I always pretend the fetish isn't a thing for me. I'm like, "Oh, look vomit, yeah that means nothing to me" or "Ewwwwww." But in my heart, vomit is my everything. When people burp I sometimes get turned on.

None of my partners have ever offered to engage in my fetish. I haven't pressed it. I don't want to see those I love suffering. I've also never pursued any of the people looking for vomitsex on various chatboards. I don't know that the smell of vomit would be sexy to me. Also, in my mind there are very specific vomit scripts that even the most well-intentioned lover would not be able to follow. Rendering one's fantasies real is a tricky business. A break in the narrative might be a grave disappointment.

Having a secret fetish has probably led me to more promiscuity in my life than I might have engaged in otherwise. Like, all my life I've been searching for that one who could trump my fantasies. I haven't found the person yet. But maybe that's how sexuality is, regardless of what direction your fantasies take.

It doesn't look like I'm ever going to get over my vomit fetish. In spite of the tape playing in my mind, I still hold a somewhat sacred sexual ideal: a union where I experience orgasm with another person based solely on what is happening in the moment, and not on what is going on in my head. I've strived for this, and while I've experienced great pleasure with others sans vomit fantasy, it's never at the level of vomit.

But there are dark, untouched corners within all of us. Sex can be very exciting in one moment and barely tepid the next. It can feel like love but not be love. It can feel like possession and then the person walks away. You can't possess another person. You can't make another person not die. If nothing else, at least my vomit fetish is mine. It's mine and it's real.

One Text Is Too Many and a Thousand Are Never Enough

I'm trying to quit getting high on people. It's really fucking hard. I'm a romantic and an addict. I crave eros, fantasy, and intrigue. I'm wired for longing. But I keep getting really sick. Longing-sick.

When you keep getting sick, you start to get tired of it. Eventually, you might be like: *This isn't working. I'm done. I want to be okay.* But it's taking me a lot of failed attempts to make any progress.

Also, getting clean off of people isn't the same as getting sober off of alcohol and drugs. Since I'm an alcoholic, there are very clear boundaries as to what I don't do. I can't text alcohol. Dealers don't send nudes. What's more, alcohol and drugs are pervasive in America, but people are even more pervasive. People are everywhere. Hot people. You can abstain from alcohol and drugs. You can't abstain from people.

I think everyone is entitled to love, even those of us seeking to quit getting high on people. But this isn't about love. This is about using people as drugs. It took me a while, but I'm beginning to get the difference. Now, when I become romantically obsessed with a person without really knowing them (or ever having met them) that signals danger for me. It's a red alert. If I feel those first fantastical pangs, I disengage.

It's sad to disengage. It's not poetic or musical. It's not what art tells me is valuable (at least the art I like). I want love at first sight to be real. But I fall in love at first sight every day. Also, love at first sext. There will never be enough sexts to sate my longing. The higher I get, the worse the comedown is.

Recently I blocked the most intense drug-people in my phone. It's been hard to do this, especially with one particular drug-person who always treated me with kindness and respect.

With this drug-person, there was genuine love. I would say we were both in love but also got fucked up on each other. So I suffered a lot, in spite of the love, because you can't make a drug-person not be a drug-person no matter how wonderful they are. What fed the drugginess was that distance, and other factors, assured we would never be able to really be together. Neither of us were really available. So we were in a constant state of longing — of almost touching — like Keats's "Ode on a Grecian Urn" but with iPhones.

The truth is, distance and unavailability — flecked with short-lived, gorgeous IRL binges —

were what made the drug-person so intoxicating. I wanted more of the drug-person than could ever be available. When I didn't get a text, I was, as junkies say, sick. When I received a text it made me well. But it only made me well until the next text I sent. Then I was waiting for him. I was sick again.

If I could be eternally and omnipotently texted, I might not have had to quit the drug-person. But no one can text you infinitely. So every day became a cycle of getting high and getting well. The only solution, as I saw it, was to quit the drug-person entirely.

I tried quitting the drug-person multiple times. But every time, I kept going back for one more taste. If I didn't go back for more, the drug-person would text me. And when the drug-person texted me I had to text back. I didn't want to "hurt him".

Was I really afraid of hurting him? I don't know. Maybe I was afraid of what he would think of me if I ignored him, that I was a "bitch" and not wonderful. Maybe I was just afraid of cutting off my supply.

Eventually, the pain of waiting for texts from the drug-person outweighed the highs. I said my final goodbye. I blocked him on my phone.

I then went through a period of grieving much deeper than I ever went through in quitting the drug-person before. I cried about deaths that happened fifteen years ago. I cried about having to grow up.

(FYI: It's probably never really about the person you think you're obsessed with. It's about old pain.)

A few weeks ago, I found myself doing really well, better than all of the times I've quit him before. When I dreamt of him, the dreams were no longer full of lust and ache. Even in my dreams I knew that we weren't right for each other. I dreamt that I flew over his apartment building in a helicopter. The building looked beautiful and he called to me to come in through the roof. But I didn't go. It's as if even my subconscious version of him was ruined. I felt glad it was ruined. I felt strong and free.

Then, the drug-person got in touch again, twice. Perhaps he sensed that I had healed and he didn't want to be forgotten. Perhaps he didn't want me to feel like I'd been forgotten. No one wants to be forgotten.

First he commented on one of my FB posts. In the past, whenever he used to do this it would get me high. But this time, when I saw the comment I was like *fuck*. I felt doom. Should I "like" it? If I didn't "like" it I would appear cold-hearted. But if I "liked" it, I'd be breaking my rule of no contact and also potentially encouraging him to contact me again. I didn't "like" it. I felt good.

A few days later, he sent me a series of messages on FB. I didn't know what to do, so I decided that

I would just ignore the messages and let them sit there forever.

This essay was supposed to be about not checking the messages. But I am a human being, so obviously that didn't work out.

I didn't check the messages for two days. Then, I went down the rabbit hole of my compulsion into a gorgeous, grammatically hellacious cascade of his drunken messages.

He said: *its incribly hard not to harass you i love you still obsivously*

He said: *i still visit your shit to sniff and i love the semlaall… in the romandic way of the beauy adnd the best…*

He said: *god i already regret this communication… howefver i must say that i huhhhh… the longer the type the lobgner i realize my mistake… i love u so much… i love ur life… i am crying… you are th e best human…. im sorry im in marrakech… i am very drunk in morroccoan country…*

It was then I realized that he, too, is probably an addict of some sort. Anyone who can meet my level of intensity can't be totally normal.

He said: *ugh… i have failed u my queen. oh i only mean to communicate that u are the best one and anything else i wish i would be vaporized for… no need to respond please… u are the only 1*

Then he said: *Please ignore me, I just want to leave you alone. Really sorry :/*

This essay was supposed to be about how I ignored him. But I am a human being, so obviously that didn't work out.

I said: *please do not throw words like this at me drunk, because i am a very sensitive human being with real feelings and am not an object (which is hypocritical because i guess i treated you like an object in some ways)*

I said: *it is very easy to tell me you love me when it is over and you are thousands of miles away in a foreign country*

I said: *could you love me at your front door?*

I said: *i don't think you could.*

I didn't think he could. And even if he said he could it wouldn't mean he could. It wouldn't mean I could. But of course I wanted him to say he could, whether or not either of us could.

He said: *i don't know what i could do which is probably a bad sign but i do miss you.*

I told him never to contact me again in any form.

Then there was a moment's pause as I thought about what I had done. *Never again in any form.* I wasn't just flushing one baggie of the drug; I was extinguishing it from my existence.

I said: *lol sorry it had to end like this*

I said: *say goodbye to me please lol*

I don't know why I kept saying *lol*. I was crying.

He said: *I'm dead now forever you can block me*

He said: *I thought I was better than drink idiocy but turns out I'm a piece of shit. oh fuck it shut up myself. bye*

It was the least satisfying ending ever. Now I want to contact him and be like, *Just one more thing!* I want to give it the perfect ending. But there will never be a perfect ending. The perfect ending is a romantic ending and thus is not an ending. The perfect ending will only feed the compulsion. So I am keeping the imperfect ending and pretending it is perfect.

But now I am sick again. I have holes in my brain where I want to hide from life. The holes are filled with voices that tell me we were nirvana, over and over. The voices seem like truth to me, because I am an addict and I want being high to be the truth. I don't know if I will ever fill the holes. But I am trying really hard not to enter them again.

Hello 911, I Can't Stop Time

I can't stop time and Los Angeles knows this. Los Angeles wants me frozen.

My spirit doesn't want me frozen. My spirit is the kind of spirit that doesn't want me to hurt myself for physical beauty, but my spirit is not an interventionist spirit unless I get quiet enough to listen to it. To be honest, I don't really want to listen to my spirt. My spirit got me into this mess of becoming human in the first place. I don't want to be human. I don't want to age or die. What I want is to be impervious to all of that. And if I can't defeat time and death, then let me at least be impervious to what other people think of me. I want to be beyond reproach. Let me at least try.

The dermatologist who will relieve me of what other people think looks like a fetus. Two months ago, when I first moved to LA, I checked in with this dermatologist, because I needed a chinzit point person. Chinzits have always been a struggle and it's best to be prepared. After re-upping some antibiotics for my chinzits, the fetus pointed out all of the sun damage on my face, particularly three lines across my forehead. He said that he could "fix those right up" with Botox.

Truth be told, the lines had bothered me for a few years but I'd never considered Botox. I didn't know anyone (or didn't think I knew anyone) who used Botox. When the fetus presented me with the Botox option I was like, *No fucking way*. I did think it was funny, however, that within one week of living in LA I was already recommended Botox.

What has changed in the two months between his recommendation and now? What made me choose to inject botulinum toxin into my face today was two months of sitting with the lines, knowing that there was a solution if I wanted it. The solution made the lines more visible. It kept speaking to me. It said: *Why suffer?* It said: *Fool them.* It said: *Fool yourself.* I almost felt as though I were being "bad" or "foolish" or "wrong" for not doing all I could to stay young-looking. I don't think this is just the American beauty industry talking. I think this is me and my fear of judgment, time, and death. Actually, maybe it is just the American beauty industry talking. Fine, then. It's loud as fuck.

The fetus takes all kinds of pictures of my face with his iPhone, asking me to smile and look grim and look sad. When we both discover that I can't properly frown, he says, *That's probably a good thing.* I don't tell him that the reason why I can't frown in front of another person is because I am overly concerned with what others think of me, and this hyperconcern has likely conditioned my face to only appear happy. It's a Pavlovian smile. Fool them, fool yourself. Same reason I'm getting Botox.

I tell the fetus not to make me look like Joan Rivers. I tell him to keep it natural. I ask him a thousand questions about the dangers of Botox and if there is any recovery time. My fear regarding my face dates back to the time I ate a box of grape candies at my grandmom's house and she spent the night scrubbing my purple tongue with a washcloth. She said she was afraid that I would have to walk down the aisle at my wedding one day with a purple tongue. Like the purple was permanent and not ephemeral.

The fetus says we're only going to do "baby Botox", just a few little squirts for the three lines. He says that there is no recovery time, but he recommends not lying down or putting my head down for three hours after the treatment. He says that in 1% of cases, someone will walk away with a "droopy eyebrow" that sags into their eyes. I know I will be the 1%. But I go ahead with it anyway.

The treatment itself takes only five minutes and is just a few needle pricks in my forehead. It's no big deal, and, looking at my face, you can't tell that I've had anything done. But upon standing up to exit and pay, I get a wave of anxiety so intense that I feel like I'm going to faint into his candy dish. A voice in my head says, *You're fucked*. It's not the voice of my god. It's my voice.

I hear the "you're fucked" voice a lot, with or without Botox. In fact, it's the "you're fucked" voice that compels me to get Botox. Only now I think I've fucked myself *because* of the Botox.

Once outside the fetus's office I immediately google "Botox death" on my phone. I text the one person I know who has admitted to having Botox and she texts me back *CHILL OUT*. I text my friend who grew up on the Upper East Side of Manhattan, but she has never had it. I feel like I have entered a new world. I am now one of "those people", the Botoxed, and can never again cross back over the threshold of the non-Botoxed. I ride my bike down the beach path and am convinced that people are staring at me. The sun sets over the Pacific and I have Botox. I stop into a store and begin "testing" my forehead in the mirror, scrunching my face and raising my eyebrows. I look insane, but my forehead appears normal. It still moves. The Botox takes three days to two weeks to really work anyway, so I won't know if I'm going to become a statue for a while. I google some more and discover that Jennifer Aniston doesn't do Botox. I am worse than Jennifer Aniston. I am worse than a lot of people.

Over the course of the next few days I feel like I have been poisoned, just a little. I have flu-like symptoms. My forehead feels like there is a plate on it. I kind of didn't realize that the word *toxin* actually means "toxin". Like, I kind of didn't think about that. I keep googling "Botox death" looking for new results. I also google "Botox flu", "Botox soulless", "plastic surgery disaster", "what's wrong with me", "why", and "how to love yourself".

As has been said, I am not a human being trying to be spiritual. I am a spiritual being having a human experience. I get it. I know that it's in there. I know that I probably contain innate coping mechanisms to deal with, and even celebrate, the ways that nature transforms my body as I age. I should probably be in some goddess circle, not the dermatologist's office. I should be processing, with a bunch of long-pubed witches, my transition from maidenhood to whatever it is that comes before crone. MILF? Pre-MILF? But I don't trust my spirit to take care of me once I leave the goddess circle. I don't trust that when I encounter another circle, a circle of superficial maidens, I won't compare myself to them and hurt.

The first time I remember my spirit trying to

tell me it would take care of me was the first time I tried psychedelics. I ate shrooms, but instead of eating them with honey, I ate them with these diet kind of Doritos made with a chemical called Olestra that makes you shit out everything. Right before I took the shrooms, I bleached my brown hair bright blond and burned my scalp. I also went to the tanning salon a hundred times. Beauty and truth are fucking confusing.

I took the shrooms in a shitty park in Massachusetts, which looked to me like Elysium. When I started tripping I was like, *Why can't people just be kind to one another?* But what I really think I meant was, *Why can't I be kind to myself?*

I knew that I was seeing truth, though later I could not tell you exactly what that truth was. What was the truth? I think the truth was my own innocence. I saw the trees of the park and that their roots were actually inverse branches and that they did not hate me. They wanted me to be deep. I swore to never hurt myself again. My spirit smiled.

But how I hurt myself so many times after that. And if that first shroom trip was a replication of the kind of psychic shift that occurs when we are dying — a few moments when we can see ourselves from the perspective of our spirit — then on my deathbed I am going to regret the ways I have hurt myself. I will regret the frivolity of chasing beauty and seeking validation, the kinds of things I have done to provide an illusion of safety on this planet, behaviors that perhaps wasted my one and only life.

If I wanted to make room for life I would probably let go of these behaviors right now. There is still time. But life is scary. Maybe I just don't want to make room for life.

One week after Botox the physical results are pretty good. The flu, headaches, and platelike feeling are gone. No droopy eyebrow. The three lines on my forehead have basically disappeared and I can still move all parts of my face. I feel like I'm tricking the world. When I see women who have forehead lines, I wonder if they "just don't know" about Botox. Then I think that maybe they do know and are actively choosing not to poison themselves. Why aren't they poisoning themselves? What's the difference between them and me — that I am game for the poison and they are not going for the poison?

The Botox will only last for three months, and I think I will probably poison myself again in the future. In fact, I know I will. Once I incorporate an element into my beauty routine, the element stays forever. I begin to rely on it to feel okay, the way my spirit wants me to rely on itself to feel okay. But it's a lot easier to rely on a tangible fix than it is to rely on a nebulous spirit, a quiet voice, deep inside yourself. I am wired to reach for shiny things. Physically, the Botox has shaved off a few years. I'm definitely fooling something. Spiritually, however, the Botox has had no positive effects. I still feel fucked a lot. I'm not whole. I'm human.

Google Hangout with My Higher Self

Me: yo

Me: r u there?

Me: i feel empty and worthless :(

Higher self: i kno

Higher self: u only come 2 me when u feel shitty

Higher self: u don't rly love me

Higher self: jk

Me: i feel like i'm not ok

Me: i feel like i'm not good

Higher self: gurl u r good

Higher self: u contain -------> infinite goodness

Me: idk

Me: i feel like plants, babies, trees, the ocean, animals, and the moon don't like me

Me: like they r talking shit or something

Me: like they can see through me and kno that i am fundamentally fucked

Higher self: ok u need 2 chill the fuck out. u need 2 sit still. u r already in the light and u don't even see it. u need 2 start sexting the light bb. send nudes 2 the light

Me: but i feel like my darkness makes me cool

Me: what if i fall in love w the light and then other ppl judge me? what if i get left alone w the light?

Higher self: being left alone w the light is the shit tho

Me: what if i get addicted to the light?

Higher self: guuuuuurl

Higher self: u have already gotten addicted 2 so much shit

Higher self: how much shit have u already gotten addicted 2 on earth?

Me: omg so much shit

Higher self: shld we go thru the list?

Me: lol no

Higher self: so maybe getting addicted 2 the light will be good addiction

Higher self: i think u will love the light! i think u have been looking for it everywhere

Me: ok. and then what happens?

Higher self: rehab!!!

Higher self: jk

Higher self: i think u cld find some freedom in it

Me: i hate freedom

Me: i'm scared of it

Me: i'm scared that i will disappear

Me: like, how will i know who i am if i am not

measuring myself against something outside me or whatev? it will all feel so bottomless and infinite. i'm ttly scared of the infinite.

Higher self: yeah the infinite is a freakshow

Higher self: u r a bad bitch who is scared of the infinite

Me: i'm a bad bitch who is scared of being alive

Me: i'm also a bad bitch who is scared of dying

Me: i feel like yoga teachers are always like "focus on the breath" but when you're dying you don't even have your breath so if you spent your whole life focusing on your breath you're kind of fucked

Me: i think what i'm most scared of is suffocating

Me: one time when i was young i was chewing a big piece of watermelon gum and the gum formed a lot of spit in my mouth and i accidentally inhaled the spit and couldn't breathe and was def choking because i couldn't cough or speak and was PETRIFIED but somehow i managed to get my air back, but like then i went to go see the movie Home Alone and the whole time at the movie theater i kept "testing" to see if i could breathe

Higher self: i kno, i wuz there

Me: why didn't u help me?

Higher self: cld u breathe?

Me: yeah

Me: but in the dark movie theater i wondered if i was in hell

Me: and every day since then i feel like i have just been testing to see if i can still breathe

Higher self: but u r still breathing, bitch

Me: yeah, but one day, the breathing really is going to stop and that is what I am scared of

Me: like, i think i am most scared of the panic i will feel when i can't breathe

Me: those moments right b4 death

Higher self: cool, i think u shld spend the rest of yr life worrying abt it

Me: :(

Higher self: actually i'm serious

Higher self: i think u don't think abt death enuff

Higher self: i think u think abt death but u don't fully *know* that u r going 2 die

Higher self: because there is no way that someone who knows they r going to die wld obsess abt the bullshit that u do

Me: can u rly *know* u r going 2 die and not be paralyzed?

Higher self: idk

Higher self: we cld try?

Higher self: i mean, you're going to die anyway so might as well

Higher self: whatev u r doing now isn't working

Me: yeah

Higher self: like, if we know one thing it's that u r definitely going to die

Higher self: so maybe it's time 2 stop worrying about bullshit

Me: but i luv bullshit

Me: bullshit makes me feel so safe

Me: like, recently i had a really bad panic attack abt capitalism and how my american lifestyle def causes suffering 4 others — humans and animals — and how i don't live up to my own consciousness of how i shld be living. like, i'm not vegan anymore so i'm evil. definitely. but then all of the chemicals that the panic attack released in my nervous system left me unhinged the following day and what did i do? i went out and bought a bunch of (definitely not vegan/ probably made in factories with not-great working conditions) stuff from nike to try to "rig up" my feels, because buying shit sometimes works — even tho this was the exact cause of my meltdown and is thus hypocritical. it makes no sense but it kind of worked. like, i'd literally been wearing the same leggings with holes in the vagina for four years and my sports bras were just my tits dangling out the bottom. so i got new sports bras and leggings. and i felt good for two seconds. but then i was like, fuck, i can't wear my new leggings with these old socks and sneakers. my toe is literally sticking out of my sneaker because the sneaker has a hole by the toe and all of the socks have holes in the same exact place. so then i started obsessing about that, but no longer felt unhinged about existential doom or how awful i am in a macrocosmic way. so i think i find obsessing abt bullshit preferable.

Higher self: tl;dr

Higher self: jk

Higher self: it seems like u r scared of containing multitudes, tbh

Higher self: like, why does it have to be all or nothing? why r u just str8 up good or str8 up evil? what if u r a v loveable douchebag? what if u r a heavenly asshole? what if u r a destructive beautiful person?

Me: idk

Me: am i allowed 2 be good and evil at the same time?

Higher self: look around, bb. that's all there is.

The Terror in My Heart Says Hi

It seems like all the cool mentally ill people are on Wellbutrin. Okay, maybe not cool, but like, my mentally ill friends.

My friend Chris said Wellbutrin is good for people like us, because instead of thinking about death for fourteen hours a day he now only thinks about it for three. It doesn't stop death, but it stops death thoughts.

My friend Lauren, a therapist who gets panic attacks while seeing patients, is on it. One time, Lauren had a panic attack so bad while seeing a patient that when the patient revealed she hadn't eaten all day, Lauren used it as an excuse for them to go outside and get a sandwich. She cloaked this exodus in teaching the patient a lesson in self-care. *You have to eat*, she said. But in her head Lauren was like, *Thank you Jesus*. If they didn't leave the room she thought she was going to die.

Okay. Wellbutrin isn't the panacea. Nothing can take away your peculiar fears and twists. But it seems like a better drug than what I'm on, which is

Effexor XR: the fucking dinosaur of antidepressants. Actually, Prozac is way older. But I still feel passé.

I've been on Effexor for about eleven years. I started taking it a year before I got sober. At first I was so fucked up that I would forget to take it half the time, or when I did take it I would get even drunker. The Effexor, coupled with the benzodiazepines I was prescribed and the opiates I was not prescribed, had me blacking out all over town.

Since I've been sober, I have chosen not to take benzos for my generalized anxiety and panic disorders. This is because benzos — Ativan, Xanax, Valium — feel so good, and are so addictive, that even nonaddict-type people often quickly get hooked on them. I don't want to awaken those receptors again.

At the same time, I don't rule out the use of benzos, should the day come that my anxiety brings me to the verge of suicide. In that case, I would have my psychiatrist prescribe me a couple of pills to get through. I know people with anxiety disorders in sobriety who take benzos as prescribed, and I wouldn't consider it a relapse if I had to do the same. For today, though, I choose not to take them. Even when shit gets really bad and my psychiatrist suggests it, I say no. I just don't want to deal with having to ask myself every time I take one if my panic attack is "severe enough" or if I am trying to get high. I feel like this would cause me more anxiety.

But Effexor has definitely been a key component of my sobriety. Psychiatrists have lowered my dosage to almost nothing when I was in periods of chemical balance and they have increased my dosage when I entered cycles of panic attacks and depression.

Two years ago my psychiatrist raised the dosage when I was finding metaphoric bats living in my chest. The increase prior to that occurred when I witnessed the death of a relative, firsthand, and you might say it "fucked me up" a little to discover, viscerally, that death is real. Both increases worked. They left me feeling more functional, less alone, less like the only people who understood me were Albert Camus and Jean-Paul Sartre (and them just barely).

I know that meds can stop working over time. Recently, my panic attacks have been so bad that I wondered if Effexor hadn't just stopped working altogether. I asked my psychiatrist about switching to a newer, sexier med. But she said we should try increasing the Effexor first. Stay with the dinosaur.

So I take more of it. I take a higher dose than I have ever taken. But I feel disappointed. It's kind of been a point of pride for me that I've never gotten close to the maximum FDA-approved dose. Like, there was always room for me to get crazier. Now

I'm inching closer to the limit. So I wonder, am I getting worse?

Then there's night sweats. Effexor gives me night sweats, which I've pretended to ignore for about eleven years. I value my mental health over my sheets, and I guess, my allure to others who might share my bed. But on the higher dose, my bed has gone from a nightly swamp to a lagoon. I already slept naked. How can I get more naked?

These questions don't matter for long. After a few weeks on the higher dose of Effexor, my psychiatrist and I agree it is no longer working at all. I feel like I'm overmedicated, but none of the right parts of me are medicated. I feel like I'm tweaking.

We decide to gradually decrease the Effexor and introduce Prozac. We do this over a series of weeks, and the transition begins very smoothly. I feel really excited that I am having less panic attacks and anxiety in general. My psychiatrist warns me that there could be withdrawal symptoms, but I don't have any. I am like, *Bitch, whatev*. I feel special and awesome for not having withdrawal symptoms.

But then, in my first week fully off the Effexor, I spin out into an anxiety hole so deep that it feels less like anxiety — or that I am dying, as I usually fear — but like I am in a battle with demons.

Maybe I should have seen this coming when,

during the first few days completely off the Effexor, I started seeing inanimate objects as dead body parts and other haunting images. I saw part of a blanket and thought it was a person's leg. I thought a black suitcase was a monster. But unless shit is really going down, I always think I can handle it. I laughed about the objects when I realized what they were. I was like, *This will be funny to tweet about.*

Then, on my fourth night off the Effexor, I awake away from home and feel what I can only describe as a darkness in my soul. It is like my soul is screaming or something is screaming in my soul. It is the terror of *Who am I? Am I bad? Is my life meaningless? What have I invested in? Why can't I breathe? Who are any of you people? And, most scarily, is there a bottom?* These are all important questions, but they don't need to be answered at three thirty in the morning in rapid-fire.

I get into a fetal position and do a "twenty-one-second countdown" technique from an ebook called *Panic Away*, where I tell the thoughts and feelings that they have twenty-one seconds to do their worst to me. I count to twenty-one over and over until I fall back asleep.

Here is an account of what happens in the days that follow:

Day 5 off Effexor

I wake up scared and I'm scared all day. I'm scared of being scared. Scared of "losing it". Scared of not being able to function. Scared of being hospitalized. Scared that I am not okay. Scared of what life is and if I am wasting mine. Scared that I have no home — that even the place I call home has no bottom to it and I will just keep falling under and under and under.

I feel self-conscious about sharing this publicly, because the feelings are so raw and immediate. But that's what So Sad Today is born from. So I tweet about it.

It's weird, you can be "so sad today" and still be scared of judgment. Like, how much mental illness is "acceptable" and how much is going to be "too much"? Someone DMs me, "We convince ourselves that we can own the identity of the anxious or depressed person. Then it sneaks up again." It's like, *I got this.* Then the mental illness is like, *No, I've got you.*

Night 5 off Effexor

A little better than the one before. I wake up once again at three thirty a.m. with the night terrors, but now I know what's going down. It's no longer an amorphous, emotional rendition of Munch's *The Scream*. It's Effexor withdrawal. Instead of spinning all the way out, I'm like, okay, these are just sensations I am feeling from the withdrawal. Don't buy into them. I go into the bathroom in the hotel room where I am staying and do some yoga poses. I haven't done yoga in years. I think *you should be doing more yoga* and *why don't you?* and *get back in the yoga game*. It feels good to be admonishing myself about yoga rather than my profound, existential badness. I feel almost excited by the experience. I'm still scared but I also feel like, *You really are strong, gurl* as I do a crappy tree pose in the mirror.

Day 6 off Effexor

All day I feel like I am on acid. Bad acid. I eat lunch in a restaurant with a painting of Marilyn Monroe on the wall. Marilyn is laughing and she looks gross and terrifying to me. She seems to be saying, *Hahahahahahaha, look how they have sold you my corpse! Look how they have sold you the American Dream, the vacation dream, any dream to distract you from asking too many questions about existence.* I'm not sure who this "they" is exactly. Maybe it's the government? Maybe it's a machine we are stuck in as we all angle for our own stuff only to become a sad girl eating in a yuppie restaurant, freaking out internally while appearing "fine" as she tries not to choke.

Then I get to a part of the "acid trip" I enjoy. I

drive out of town, into the desert, and walk around on some rocky-desert thingy. For a few minutes, I feel like everything is going to be okay and that I am okay, because the wide-open space won't judge me. I feel wild and alive. I take some of the rocks with me, even though whenever I take "spiritual souvenirs" they never end up holding the same magic and it's better to just keep experiences like that in your heart maybe.

But mostly, it's hard to enjoy the faux–acid trip because I keep running into the same fears I had when I used to take psychedelics for real, like, *What if this feeling never goes away?* and *What if I'm like this forever?* I'm always scared that every feeling is going to be permanent.

Day 7 off Effexor

No night terrors last night, but then the day is awful. I try to watch stand-up comedy in bed and suffocate. Mostly, I am just exhausted. I am exhausted from dealing with this and exhausted from trying to convince myself that I'm not dying. My friend says that whenever I start to feel weird I should just say to myself that I'm sick, but I'm going to get better. I keep making these strange sounds just to make sure I'm still alive and breathing. I hope this shit has a happy ending.

Day 8 off Effexor

I am scared. It's fear on top of all the fear chemicals that are being released in me. They are just like *whoosh* and it is very hard (impossible) not to believe you are dying, or about to lose it, when your body is having a chemical terror response. I am looking for evidence to reflect my feelings back to me. My chemicals are like, *DANGER! Doom!* I feel alone and angry and scared. My head is like, *What if I fucked myself changing the meds and I'm never okay again?*

Day 9 off Effexor

I wake up in a panic, covered in sweat and stinking. I jump in the bath and then go back to sleep. I have a dream about the person who I may never fully get over. In the dream, he goes down on me with a pacifier in his mouth. I come really quickly.

I try to answer my "what if" questions with "so what" answers that diffuse them.

What if this is the wrong medication?
So what, I'll just work with my psychiatrist until we find the right one.

What if I want to sleep forever and can't stop sleeping?
Okay, so then you sleep the rest of your life. You've

done a lot already in your life. You've probably done enough.

What if these butterflies in my stomach never go away?
Good. I think you should just vomit all over the floor. Just keep vomiting. It's fine.

I am desperate. I buy a blue crystal from a New Age store that's said to "bring serenity". I know that I officially live in California because I'm carrying around a crystal in my bra. I reach in, while driving, and feel around to check and make sure it is still there. Some bro looks over and thinks I am feeling myself up. Good for him.

Day 10 off Effexor
I call my psychiatrist. I tell her that I'm feeling surging anxiety. She says there's no way I'm in Effexor withdrawal anymore. Maybe I am on too much Prozac? She tells me to decrease the Prozac.

My friend gives me a tarot card reading and says that I am going to be fine. While she is reading the cards, I have a panic attack. She points to a card called "Strength" that shows a woman taming a lion and a card called "The Fool" with some dude dancing on the edge of a cliff without falling off. I feel like I am not taming the lion. I feel like the lion is attacking me. Also, I think I am going to fall off the cliff.

Day 11 off Effexor

I call my psychiatrist again, even though I don't want to be a nuisance. Now she thinks I might not be on enough Prozac. She tells me to increase the Prozac.

I talk to this crazy girl. She tells me that people with anxiety shouldn't take Prozac and that I should get off it or I will go "over the edge". She says that I live in California now and I should just "green juice it". This is one of those girls who doesn't stop talking shit or gossiping. The only thing she knows about meds is that her sister works in pharmaceutical sales. I feel tempted to take her medical advice.

Other people give me advice too. *Don't go back on Effexor, ride it out, it might take months but you can do it, I believe in you!* I don't believe in me. Not at all. Everyone thinks I'm going to be okay except me.

Day 12 off Effexor

I'm going back on fucking Effexor.

Day 13 off Effexor

I'm not going back on fucking Effexor.

Day 14

I'm driving my car on the highway and I have to take a shit. There is nowhere to pull over. For the first time in ten days, I experience a sensation more powerful than the anxiety. I feel grateful for the feeling of having to take a shit and having nowhere to take it. I am like, *Yes*. I feel like myself. But then I take the shit. And the anxiety returns.

I go to a work-related meeting. This dude is talking about sports. He goes through every sport before he even gets to the matter at hand. He does basketball, football, baseball, hockey. He even does golf. I am scared my head is going to pop off. I'm not even there. But what's scarier than the feeling in the meeting is the feeling after the meeting. Usually, when I am in an anxiety-inducing situation, I experience relief as soon as I leave. But when I leave the meeting, there is no respite. Golf dude is gone but I am draped in a thick, gray, pulsating cloud.

Day 15

I'm going back on fucking Effexor.

Never Getting Over the Fantasy of You Is Going Okay

Is fake love better than real love? Real love is responsibility, compromise, selflessness, being present, and all that shit. Fake love is magic, excitement, false hope, infatuation, and getting high off the potential that another person is going to save you from yourself.

Of course, nobody can save you from yourself. But it's easy to ignore that reality. Simply project your own romantic ideation, childhood wounding, and overactive fantasy life onto another human being. Even better if the person possesses fewer inner resources than you. Like, the less basic coping skills possessed by the object of your obsession, the better the fake love.

One form of romantic obsession is to become infatuated with someone who actually exists. With this type of romantic obsession, you project your entire fantasy narrative onto a person in your life and attempt to get them to comply. You take a living, breathing human being and try to stuff them into the insatiable holes inside you. These holes are in no way shaped like that person (or any person). But you believe that this fantasy person will fill you, because he or she possesses all the imaginary qualities you seek in a lover. And how do you know that he or she possesses all of these qualities? You put them there.

Another form of romantic obsession is to fall in fake love with a person who doesn't exist at all. With this type of romantic obsession, you fall in love with a magic hologram of a person you create based on a distant image. This image may be of a dead person, an online-only person, a famous person, or a cartoon. But he or she cannot be a flesh person whom you actually encounter in waking life. In this version of romantic obsession, the hope is that if a magic hologram falls in love with you, then you are magic too. The longing is hope. It keeps you alive.

I once had a hot affair with a Twitter avatar for over two years. The avatar was shadowy and brooding — a total omega male. His tweets were those of an enfant terrible: words of disdain for the contemporary electronic music scene juxtaposed with nihilist philosophy, and also, his dick. I wanted to be mysterious and ghostly like him. I wanted a mysterious and ghostly dick. If I couldn't physically have my own dick, I would claim the dick of the avatar. If I could not be the terrible boy, I would be the ingénue, the good witch with shadow dick in hand.

I began subtweeting spells. I conjured a narrative

wherein I, with my magic tweets (and pussy), was the only one who could penetrate the darkness of the avatar. Soon the avatar followed me back and I convinced myself that he was in love with me. Now, every time he tweeted, I was sure that he was definitely tweeting to me. Something about Coachella and his dick. Me. Something vaguely Nietzschean and his dick. Me. When the avatar faved one of my tweets, I contacted a psychic for advice. Was it a love match? She recommended a therapist. When the avatar faved two of my tweets in a row, it felt like fucking.

Eventually the person behind the avatar came to New York City, where I was living, to play music. During his set I watched his hands on the turntables, hypnotized. The club was dark and I was so turned on. These were my avatar's hands!

But after the show, I discovered that the man behind the avatar was just a regular person. He was blond, not shadowy, and very Midwestern. I sat at the bar with the man behind the avatar. We talked about Twitter and I watched him get sloppy drunk. He ate a pound of pork fried rice. I thought the spell was broken.

The next day, back on Twitter, the avatar began speaking to me again in its sexy way. *My dick my dick fuck everything my dick.* The real man behind the avatar may have just been a man, but I wanted the avatar more than ever. And I wanted to know if the avatar wanted me.

Impulsively, I sent a text message to the person behind the avatar. Specifically, I said, *SEND ME A LOCK OF YOUR HAIR.* The person behind the avatar was confused. Communication ceased. Tweets were no longer faved. No lock of hair was sent. I found out he had a girlfriend. Now, the fantasy was no longer a safe place for me to "hang out" in my head. It was a painful place.

I'm not sure what makes us willing to try to let go of a fantasy person, other than finally being in enough pain and just being like, *Okay. I want to surrender the ghost.*

But getting over the fantasy of a person (especially the fantasy of a fantasy person) is hard. I've been romantically obsessed with so many people that I've kind of become a getting-over-the-fantasy-of-people athlete. Here are some of the tactics I've incorporated into my training, the ones that worked and the ones that didn't:

1. Conducting "research" by checking the person's Twitter, FB, Tumblr, and Instagram every second, all the while feeling proud that at least you aren't "liking" and faving their shit anymore.

What are you doing? Stop doing this. Close all the

tabs right now. If you feel like you absolutely can't stop, try abstaining for thirty days. Or seven. Count the days.

Once you abstain from checking their social media, you will enter a short period of withdrawal. This is because you aren't getting that hit of dopamine from seeing the person's face pop up — or that shot of adrenaline from the sudden appearance of a mystery person in their selfies. You're eliminating what may feel like your last connection to them.

But what you're also getting is a reprieve from that emotional hangover every time they tweet something good (note: the tweets are never that good, you just want them to be). Soon you are going to feel really free.

If you really love yourself, you will block and unfollow the person on all social media. But if you really love yourself you probably aren't reading this essay. So let's take it slow.

2. Giving the person a new nickname amongst your friends, like "heroin" or "pancake ass" or "teletubby", and only referring to the person with this nickname.

Yes. This is one of the best ways to "reframe" the image of a person in your mind. Sometimes we don't want to give up our idea of a person, because it provides us with a beautiful place to go in our heads

— even when that beauty is painful. Well, laughter is beautiful too. I fully encourage you to impale that vampire on the cross of his tiny penis, simply by giving the tiny penis a name.

3. Writing down the person's name on a piece of paper and throwing it into a fire, or any other type of "magic goodbye surrendering ritual".

Eh. This can be freeing for, like, ten seconds. It's exciting when a thirty-dollar candle promises to eliminate the memory of a person forever. But it's unrealistic to suspect that you'll surrender the entire fantasy of a person and never go there mentally again. And if the candle doesn't work, you might stop believing in magic. I think it's important to never stop believing in magic.

4. Having sex with them again "one last time".

There is no last time.

5. Having sex with someone else (or multiple people) immediately after having sex with the fantasy person to avoid the "come-down" off of sex with the fantasy person but sort of sustain the emotional high.

This can be powerful, in a fake way, like being the militaristic dictator of your own sex nation. But you're probably going to end up comparing the second person to your fantasy person. Usually, the second person won't be able to live up to the fantasy person and it'll just be sad.

It should be noted that this tactic can work really well on the rare occasion that the second person is as hot and amazing as the fantasy person (or at least, you perceive them to be). But be warned: This tactic can backfire if you end up getting hooked on the second person too. There's nothing worse than waiting for texts from two (or even three) fantasy people and not hearing from any of them.

6. Getting into a relationship with someone else who you don't even like and pretending that new person is the fantasy person while you are having sex with them.
Relationship experts say that fantasizing about one person while fucking another person is natural and normal. But it's one thing to fantasize about someone you've never had feelings for, and it's another to be reenacting *Wuthering Heights* in your head with an old lover while fucking a totally new lover. For me this has only resulted in crying during sex. And not in a good way.

7. Trying to "stay friends".
You have enough friends.

Do you really want to just be friends? There is

nothing worse than just being friends with someone you're in love with who isn't in love with you. Actually, being friends with benefits with someone you're in love with who isn't in love with you is worse. But friendship with no benefits is bad too.

You'll know when (if ever) it's finally time to be friends with the fantasy person if they text you and it's just boring and annoying, rather than intoxicating. Like your real friends.

8. Changing the person's name in your phone to *DO NOT CONTACT* or *STOP* or the toilet emoji.

I'm a very slow learner and I don't like being told what to do — not even by me. The little warnings I leave for myself on my phone never seem to deter me in the moment of bad decision making. I've sexted with the word *STOP* for hours. I've declared my love for a toilet emoji.

But this method will probably work for some of you, and I encourage you to try it. Maybe try using the cop car emoji.

9. Reading the other person's horoscope to see what's going on in his life and if he is ever coming back to you.

No. Stop doing this. Also, let's take a break from reading the love section of your horoscope. Also, let's stop googling "how to seduce Aries" and "how to make Aries man fall in love with you". For the record, I think Aries men should just be avoided entirely. Aries women are fine though.

10. Going to a psychic.

Depends on the psychic and depends on what they say. If they say that the fantasy person is your "soul mate", you're fucked.

11. Talking to your craziest friends about their love problems.

Yes! Pick your craziest friend. Ask her about some douchebag she is obsessed with. Watch her try to turn the douchebag into a knight. Observe her inability to see that person as he really is, because if she did, she'd have nothing to obsess about.

Be grateful. You may be in a shitty place, but you aren't as crazy as her. Remember that you have the potential to be that crazy if you don't let go of the fantasy person.

12. Get a mantra.

Mantras have saved my ass so many times. If you have an overactive mind like mine, it's very hard to continually deflect your thoughts away from the fantasy person if you don't immediately have a replacement thought on deck. Definitely get a mantra. As soon as you catch yourself thinking about the person (even if it's hours in), go to the mantra.

Different mantras work for different people. Some people like doing positive affirmations, but those just make me feel like a loser. Instead, I prefer weirder, trippier, psychedelic mantras and prayer mantras so I feel more like a space cowgirl than someone who is trying to tell herself she is *worthy*, *whole*, and *loved*.

13. Therapy.

I feel like therapy doesn't really work, but that's only because I've been in therapy my whole life and I'm not perfect or "fixed", so I'm always like, *Therapy is stupid*.

That being said, I can't imagine not being in therapy. I may never become a completely whole person, but I might have a shot at becoming three-fourths of a person. Three-fourths of a person isn't bad.

Final assessment: Therapy is stupid and annoying, but it works just well enough that you should still do it. Definitely get help.

14. Become totally obsessed with the fantasy of someone else.

Don't do this. But obviously, you're going to do this and so am I.

Keep Your Friends Close but Your Anxiety Closer

Something weird happened. A person said that he was sorry to hear I'm still having panic attacks. He hopes I feel better soon.

It was weird to hear someone express sympathy for mental illness in the way that they might for physical illness. I mean, I know my panic disorder is an illness. I take medicine for it (an SSRI). I see doctors: a psychiatrist monthly and a therapist weekly. The symptoms are palpable. Like a person living with chronic pain, I view every area of my life through the filter of visceral anxiety. From the sensation of suffocating to dizziness and dissociation, my entire nervous system is involved — adrenal glands included. Scientifically, this shit is real.

But there is something about the classification of panic disorder as a mental condition, rather than a purely physical one, that prevents me from extending compassion to myself. If it were solely physical, I might be nicer to me. I might actually have some self-love.

Instead I play the tape of "you're so fucked".

I even buy into some antiquated notions around mental illness that it is "all in my head" or that I am "imagining it".

Well, so what if it were all in my head? I'd still be suffering. Would I not deserve compassion and self-love? Intellectually I'm like, *Yeah*. But emotionally I'm like, *No fucking way. Buck up, gurl.*

Even writing the word *self-love* makes me feel stupid. Is anything more bullshit, kale-eating, juice-fasting contemporary American than the notion of self-love? "Be gentle with yourself, you deserve it." Do I really?

My feelings of shame around the condition create a drive in me to overcompensate, overachieve, and never appear vulnerable. These then serve as a catalyst for the condition. I put pressure on myself to perform like a completely healthy person, lest people find out that I am "not okay". I don't take sick days. I fear my condition and its implications for my life. I'm like *something is very wrong with me* and then I'm like *what the fuck is wrong with me that I feel like something is wrong with me?* None of this is good for the nervous system.

Like, right now I'm scared that I'm not being funny in this essay. I'm not wearing my mask, the one that lets you know that shit is fucked up yet also under control. The mask says: *You don't have to worry about me. I've still got it together enough to get outside the anxiety and be funny. I'm safe.*

Recently, a woman said she likes my writing because I'm not a whiny cunt. I think what she means is that she likes my funny mask. But now, the panic attacks are stripping me of my ability to not be a whiny cunt. I want to be in control of my whiny cunt levels! If I'm going to alienate you, I want to curate that alienation. I want to craft the persona that turns you off. I don't want the real me, my vulnerabilities and humanity, to leak out and make you run. I don't want to have needs.

Like, what if you found out I am really not okay? What if you knew that I am suffering a lot right now and really scared? Would you flee? I don't want to find out. So I deflect my vulnerability into humor or "wise platitudes".

That's what I did when the person extended his kind words. I was like, *Oh, well, our curses are our blessings. If I didn't have a panic disorder there would be no So Sad Today.*

That's sort of true. I mean, So Sad Today wouldn't exist if I never experienced emotional and psychic pain that felt like it was going to kill me. And I like that So Sad Today exists. But it's also sad that I am afraid to just say thank you, human to human, when someone extends sympathy. Like, to receive compassion means I am weak. And I am terrified of being weak.

I'm also terrified of other people's narratives. I don't want to be perceived as falling apart. Like, it's fine that I'm frightened of me. But if you are frightened of me, then the problem is more real. I don't really know how much I am allowed to fall apart. I don't think I want to find out.

At the same time, I kind of do want to find out. After all these years of preserving my facade in daily life, I'm fucking tired. It would probably be a real relief to just crumble. I wish I could trust that the universe has me and that I could just let go. Or, like, even if I don't trust that the universe has me (and I don't), it would be a relief to just surrender anyway. I think my biggest fear and deepest wish is to surrender.

Like, I would love to just stand up at a work meeting and be like, "Hi, I'm sorry, I can't do this. I may be talking about 'our brand' but I'm definitely dying. You are too. We all are. But, like, I think I am dying right now. My throat is closing in and my chest is constricted. I have to go. I don't want to die here."

I would love to tell a creative collaborator, "Hey, I know that you want to talk about narrative arc. But I'm actually not inside my body anymore. Did you know that in my head you are the enemy? You have become the enemy, because you've trapped me inside this Starbucks."

I'd like to tell a friend, "I have more panic attacks around you than anyone else. I am supposed to feel comfortable around you, and the fact that I am supposed to be comfortable adds to my shame around not being comfortable. This makes me anxious. I think we should just text for the rest of the friendship. Thanks."

I'd like to tell a lover, "The panic attacks I have around you are more painful than the ones I have around anyone else. This is because I am supposed to feel intimate with you. The pressure to feel close to you, while I am having a panic attack, makes me feel totally and completely alone."

It's probably good that I don't say these things to people. It's probably good that I keep pushing myself to leave the house and maintain my social masks of competence, engagement, and comfort. But what if I did tell people exactly what was going on? What if I valued my own peace of mind more than what other people think of me? Would I end up jobless, friendless, and loveless? Would I vanish entirely?

One time I saw an interview with a female musician whom I greatly admire, someone who is known to suffer from mental illness. She is brilliantly talented and has exhibited some eccentric behavior over the years, including a few rather public breakdowns. She contains madness and talent. She contains both of those things.

The interviewer asked her about her typical day. He was like, "Do you wake up and make breakfast? Do you make some eggs?" She looked at him coldly and responded, "I don't eat eggs."

At that moment I realized that the one question I would want to ask her, the only question for me worth asking, would be "Is it worth being so talented if you also have to suffer from a profound sensitivity that is intrinsically connected to your gifts?"

But I don't know if she could even answer. What if she wants to possess her talent and also to be free of torment. What if she doesn't want to have to choose. I think it's okay to not be grateful for your curses. I think it's okay to just want your blessings to be blessings.

I Told You Not to Get the Knish: *Thoughts on Open Marriage and Illness*

I have never told the story of my husband's illness. His illness is not my illness, and so I did not think it was my story to tell. But the illness is a third party in our relationship. I have been in a relationship with the illness for eleven years. So in this way, perhaps, it is my story too.

In the past, my husband has said that he would prefer not to be a subject of my writing. But he has also said that he would never want to censor me. He says, *Do what you need to do for art*.

Poetry is art.

Is an essay art?

I asked my husband if I have his permission to write about him and his illness in prose.

He said, *Just make sure you give me a really big penis.*

He also asked that I change his name to Ron Jeremy, so that he may have some autonomy — some distance — from this essay.

Ron Jeremy felt like family from the first time we met. I was a suburban Jew, and he was an

Italian American from a Catholic family — raised in Queens — but I immediately sensed in him an essential simpatico that made him seem Jewish (in the same ways that I felt Jewish) or more Jewish (in the ways that seemed important) than any Jewish boy I'd been with. He was warmer, funnier, more neurotic and verbose than any of them. He had read more books than all of them combined. He called himself a custodian of words. He was menschy.

The first thing I ever said to Ron Jeremy was, *Shut up this is my game.* I was day-drunk, as I always was then, leading a drinking game at my weekly East Village party. The party was called Drinkers with Writing Problems. Ron Jeremy had come with a friend of a friend to meet girls. He met me.

Ron Jeremy says that he took one look at me and knew I was the sexually liberated Jewish girl of his dreams. Twenty minutes after we met, we made out in a photo booth. But before I kissed him, I told him he had to take me on a real date the next day.

The following afternoon we went to the Second Avenue Deli. It was still on Second Avenue then, and not yet a bank. Ron Jeremy got matzoh ball soup, which I told him was kind of goyish. I got gefilte fish.

Afterward, we sat on a bench with the pigeons pooping around us and kissed. I felt safe with him, also excited. He had impeccable taste in music and books, and a lot of integrity when it came to bullshit. He didn't wear a hipster costume, as he called it. Also, he was ten years older than me. For a man and woman, this put us at the same maturity level.

Ron Jeremy told me that he would be going to Paris for ten days. He asked if I would go to a concert with him when he returned. The joke between us now is that at the time he was putting the "pussy on lockdown". We emailed every day he was away.

When Ron Jeremy got back he brought me a framed photo of a grave he'd found at Père Lachaise Cemetery that had my last name on it. We went out and got drunk, then went back to his apartment, which was in Stuyvesant Town — a sort of middle-class housing project in the East Village. I was scared walking in. Stuyvesant Town had an Auschwitz aesthetic, and all of the redbrick buildings looked the same. I was like, *How do I get out of here if I need to?* He showed me the escape route on Avenue B and I felt safer. Also, I liked his apartment immediately. It had a retro seventies vibe, everything brown and velvet. It reminded me of my favorite grandmom's apartment.

There has always been a mother-daughter relationship between Ron Jeremy and me. If we knew each other in a past life, he was definitely my grandmother or mother. I have no daddy issues to speak of. If anything, our ten-year age difference reflects only my mommy issues.

Ron Jeremy and I fooled around that night in his brown bed. We didn't fuck. I don't remember exactly what we did sexually. But I remember all the freckles on his back. I remember being able to sleep easily next to him. I also remember eating bagels with him in the apartment the next morning. That's how it was with us. We were bagels, before we were hot sex.

The first time I saw Ron Jeremy get sick was a year into the relationship, just before a trip we took to New Orleans. He had a high fever and mono symptoms: sweating, swollen glands, extreme exhaustion and weakness, seasickness, an inability to regulate his body temperature. He faked enough health to take the trip. In New Orleans, I didn't even realize he was still sick. He hid it from me in muffaletta sandwiches and strawberry daiquiris. Only later did it hit me that he didn't want to ruin what was still a fairly new relationship.

The illness had been a catalyst in the destruction of a prior relationship. When Ron Jeremy was with Nina, his last girlfriend, a strange fever had come upon him and left him bedridden for months. The stress of an ongoing illness — the depression, repetition, and paralysis of it — can be too much for some people. It was for Nina.

At that time, Ron Jeremy was tested for every disease — HIV, cancer, hepatitis, diabetes, lupus, MS — but doctors could not find anything. The only thing they found, in months of testing, was slightly elevated liver enzymes. He called it his mystery liver ailment. Then the illness went away and he didn't think about it again. Then he met me.

The winter after our New Orleans trip, Ron Jeremy got sick again. This time he stayed sick. He was housebound, bedridden mostly, for three months.

I tried to cure him with soup. I made him chicken soup, harkening back to my Jewish ancestors. I was a shitty nurse, but the soup was real. There were bones in it, and dill. It did nothing for him.

He was scared. I had no idea what to do. I do not come from nurturers. In my family, you got up and went to school unless you were vomiting or had a fever. Ron Jeremy's fever waxed and waned. At least it was tangible. His other symptoms — the weakness that rendered him unable to walk from the bed into the living room, the brain fog he described — were so nebulous to me. He couldn't even read.

Then, one day in spring, after months in his pajamas, Ron Jeremy got better. We pretended he would never be sick again. We went to Coney Island

and roller coastered. We ate sushi outside the walls of the apartment. We saw PJ Harvey at the Knitting Factory. We walked in Tompkins Square Park and went to parties. Then, he got sick again.

This is a pattern that would repeat over and over. In the years that followed, Ron Jeremy would be healthy for long stretches — sometimes for nine months at a time. During those periods we ignored the mystery illness. We buried it. On the chatboards we frequented, there were people desperate to figure out what was wrong with them. But when Ron Jeremy was well we left those people behind. The illness would become a shadow from the past. If you touched it, or got too close, it could get on you. So we stayed away.

Then, inevitably, Ron Jeremy would get sick again. He would "fall in the hole", as he called it. Bedridden. And every time he became bedridden, he stayed there for months. It would take him ninety days to get from bedridden to mobile again.

When he was sick, it felt like he would never be well again. I would float between two realms: the outside world of mobility and sunlight, and the apartment world of darkness, heavy air, fear, and desperation.

I grew up thinking that doctors could fix anything. Like, there had to be a diagnosis and there had to be a cure. When Ron Jeremy was sick, we saw doctors. But he got tested and retested and came up negative for everything. We were ready to buy whatever theory was sold to us. But there weren't any.

This is my one and only life, said Ron Jeremy. *What is happening?*

Then, we went to a new immunologist who ran different types of blood tests. She told us that the elevated liver enzymes were a symptom, not a cause. She diagnosed him with CFIDS/ME: umbrella terms for people with various types of chronic neuroimmune diseases. In Ron Jeremy's case, she was able to trace his illness to a heavy viral load and his overactive detector cells. Also, most important, he suffered from an extreme deficit of killer cells. His body did not fight infection like normal people. His immune system was broken.

As I understand it, the human immune system has three types of cells. There are detector cells, which suss out illness. There are messenger cells, which send a message that the body has been invaded with illness. And there are killer cells, which receive the message and fight off the illness. In patients with HIV, it is the messenger cells that are broken. Ron Jeremy's messenger cells were fine. But his detector cells were paranoid, neurotic, obsessing about everything: traces of old illnesses, old colds. They were neurotic Jewish mothers. But when the neurotic Jewish mothers attempted to relay their barrage of messages, there was no one to relay them to. The killer cells weren't there, and the ones that were didn't do any killing.

Maybe Ron Jeremy's killer cells were tired of being nagged and so they left. Or maybe Ron Jeremy's neurotic Jewish mother cells only nagged so much because they felt they were shouting into the void. They were talking to themselves.

The immunologist was named Sue. Sue had been dealing with various types of chronic neuroimmune diseases since the eighties: chronic Lyme, Epstein-Barr. She told me that I was not at risk of contracting his disease — that it was not sexually transmitted. She also said that no one had found a cure yet.

Sue was willing to try a vast array of treatments — some of which had shown some effect on patients she had seen, and some of which we found on chatboards. We called her Sue the pooh-pooher, because she never got too excited about one treatment. Later, we learned to appreciate Sue's skepticism.

If you tell a desperate person with an incurable illness that you can cure him, he will believe you. Sue never promised to cure Ron Jeremy, but others did. Some doctors were well-intentioned, just very far out there. Others oversold their own treatments, made grandiose promises, and loved the sounds of their own voices.

In the years we've been together, Ron Jeremy has spent thousands of dollars on treatments. He has tried everything from the most toxic Western drugs to traditional Eastern medicine to the most woo-woo hippie treatments. There was amoxicillin, Valcyte, Valtrex, Nexavir, and Provigil. I've injected him with human growth hormone, vitamin B12, and Gc-MAF: a protein-derived macrophage.

Though he does not have HIV, he has done a course of two HIV drugs — Viread and Isentress — simultaneously. The hypothesis with these drugs was that if one part of his immune system was compromised, perhaps the drugs that treated an alternate part of his immune system would have some effect. There was no effect.

He has done testosterone patches and prednisone, green tea extract, St. John's wort, fish oil, iron supplements, and ginseng.

There was a heavy course of Chinese medicine with Dr. Lu: acupuncture three times a week for six months and multiple herbs.

There was the salmon and salad diet care of Dr. H, the Paleo diet via Dr. J, gluten-free, dairy-free, sugar-free, and every other elimination diet.

There were blood protein infusions via Dr. E.

There was a vitamin drip, coenzyme Q-10, probiotics, some mushroom pill.

There was a coffee enema, wherein Ron Jeremy lay spread eagle on our bathroom floor with his ass in the air and I shot a pot of coffee into his asshole via an enema bag and a tube.

Ron Jeremy has engaged in mindfulness, meditation, and mindfulness meditation.

He has seen psychologists and psychiatrists, tried Effexor and Lexapro.

We moved from Manhattan to Brooklyn.

There was helminthic therapy — worm therapy — wherein we grew worms in his friend's feces in a Tupperware container in our bathroom. We applied them to Ron Jeremy's skin like a salve. He might have had a minor psychedelic experience, but no improvement in health.

The year 2008 was particularly bad. Ron Jeremy was housebound for seven months straight and we were engaged to be married. The day we went to pick up the ring from an antiques jeweler in Midtown, he met me there in a cab: sweating, shaking, and feverish.

It is not an easy decision to marry a person with a disease like this no matter how much you love him. I had always shielded my parents from the true severity of Ron Jeremy's illness. I remember shopping for a wedding dress with my mom and thinking I just can't do this. I remember crying quietly in the dressing room until she asked to be let in.

This was when I finally conveyed to her the seriousness of Ron Jeremy's condition. Both of my parents encouraged me to reconsider my decision. They had always liked Ron Jeremy, but what kind of life was I signing on for? They were scared. Did I know what I was getting myself into? I did and I didn't.

I also had other adults in my life, one mentor in particular, who encouraged me not to make a decision based on fear. Ultimately, I chose to marry Ron Jeremy because, I reasoned, I would rather be with Ron Jeremy sick than another man healthy.

Does anyone really know who they are marrying? People change. We do not know if the person we commit to will be the same person in ten years. We do not know who he or she will become. Will you be the same person in ten years: in health, body, money, interests, mental health?

Ron Jeremy and I did not know at the time that his illness was progressive. We considered him an anomaly, lucky even, as some people with this disease are bedridden year-round. But over the years we have been married, Ron Jeremy's relapses have become more and more frequent, to the point that he is never not sick. Those windows of health are gone. His lows are no longer so low that he cannot make it from the bed into the kitchen (or maybe he is just more used to coping). But now, even at his best, he cannot walk more than a few blocks without stopping and resting. He looks for benches and walls. He plots routes. Now instead of sick and well he floats between sick and sicker.

The saddest part of the illness for me to watch is the brain fog that gets in the way of Ron Jeremy doing the things he loves: reading great works of fiction, and writing. He reads some, but not with the voraciousness he once enjoyed. He doesn't really write.

Had I known that his illness would only continue to get worse, I am not sure if my decision would have been different. At the time we got married, I didn't know how much the illness would impact my life. I didn't know that we would move four thousand miles across the country to Los Angeles, where the climate is easier on a sick person. I didn't know how many events I would attend alone, unpartnered.

I didn't know how long a haul the illness would be, how monotonous and seemingly hopeless sometimes. I didn't know that the illness would be another body in the marriage — always present, even when we are not together. When I am out with friends, living my life, as Ron Jeremy has always encouraged me to do, the illness speaks to me and says I should be home. But sometimes I do not want to go home, because the illness — and its resulting depression — fill all the rooms of my home. Even when Ron Jeremy isn't depressed, the illness itself is a palpable depression.

In the months leading up to our wedding, Ron Jeremy started a course of hydrocortisone. It is the only thing that has ever really worked. And while hydrocortisone is more of a bandage, and not meant to be a long-term treatment, in the fall of 2008 and for much of 2009 he lived like a healthy person. We traveled to Spain. We traveled to Rome. I remember skipping toward him in a medieval courtyard in Barcelona like, *Look! We are still children!* Once again, we pretended that the illness no longer existed. Then the hydrocortisone stopped working. He has not been healthy since.

Living with a sick person puts me in touch with some of my greatest fears. One of those fears is being still with myself. Like, I am scared to be still for Ron Jeremy — to be present for him at his most paralyzed — because it forces me to be still with myself. Another one of my fears is boredom, hopelessness, the feeling that I am dead while I am alive. The thing about chronic illness is that it's so fucking boring. The sick person gets depressed and you get depressed. If you're lucky, you share a dark sense of humor.

In Ron Jeremy's and my case, that means we joke about suicide. We call it the miracle of suicide. When Ron Jeremy feels suicidal, as anyone in his position might, I tell him that there can only be one suicidal person in the family. And sorry, it's me.

Ron Jeremy describes the experience of his illness as shameful. I'm always perplexed as to why he would feel shame, as the illness is not something he brought on himself. It is not his fault. But the thing is, I feel ashamed too. Sometimes I feel like having a sick husband is a measure of my worth. Like, of course I would get the husband who is sick. Of course I am not good enough to have married a healthy person.

Sometimes, when I see my friends' boyfriends or husbands, I am amazed at what they can do. They can carry babies. They can make plans and not cancel them. But I don't want any of those men. I still want Ron Jeremy.

The nebulous nature of this particular illness can be shameful too. People want to get their minds around it. The fact that it's not a "brand-name" illness, something easily defined, means I have to answer all kinds of weird questions.

Like, with other diseases, you don't have to

explain the disease. People just go, "I'm so sorry." They get it immediately. But instead, we get well-meaning people thinking they are doctors. *Has he tried acupuncture? I'm tired all the time too, I wonder if I have it. It might be celiac. It might be candida. Does he drink green juice? Are you sure it isn't just depression? I heard this thing on NPR. I heard this thing on PBS.*

If Ron Jeremy had cancer, people probably wouldn't tell me that a gluten-free diet is the cure. Sometimes, I wonder if people even believe his illness is real. Sometimes, because of his absence in so many of my activities, I wonder if they think my husband is imaginary.

It sounds fucked up, but I get jealous of people whose partners have brand-name illnesses. There is no rubber bracelet for Ron Jeremy's illness (not that I would wear one, because that shit is ugly). There are no walkathons. No fund-raisers. Ron Jeremy, himself, has said that he feels he would be better off with HIV. At least there are treatments that work.

I don't want to be defined by Ron Jeremy's illness. I don't want people to ask me how he is doing when I see them. I pretend to people, especially to myself, that this isn't hard. I don't want pity. I want to be happy and have a good life. I don't want to be sad. Or, I want to be sad about the things that I choose to be sad about. But I guess that is not how life works.

Sometimes I feel full of despair and cannot figure out why. Like I forget to equate the two things: the illness and the sadness. Then I wonder why I am sad. Then I get scared that my sadness is a free-floating sadness that will never go away. Sometimes I feel doomed.

I think I live with an awareness of illness that extends beyond what most married people my age have had to deal with. The illness puts me in touch daily with mortality and reality and darkness. I think about death a lot. I think about how Ron Jeremy will someday be dead and so is, in a way, already dead. I think about my own fragility and that I, too, will someday be dead. In universe time, I am already dead.

I want to hide from the monotony and darkness of the illness in the levity of something else: something frivolous, something young. I want to feel young, because the illness exacerbates the ten-year age difference between Ron Jeremy and me. I want to feel young, because the illness reminds me that time is passing for me too. I am vain. I'm scared of aging.

When we had been together for five years, just before we got married, Ron Jeremy and I decided to experiment with nonmonogamy. This wasn't a direct result of the illness, though I think it played a role. When you're sick all the time, you want to seize the moments when you are well and squeeze all the juice out of them you can. When your partner is sick, you want frivolous joy.

Ron Jeremy was going to Rio for a friend's bachelor party. He told me that there were brothels there, brothels that functioned like clubs. I sort of encouraged him to go. I was like, *I really don't think I would mind if you had that experience*. Like, I really felt I would be okay with it. And it turned out I was.

But I had a question for him. If Ron Jeremy got to go to Rio, and have the full Rio, then what did I get?

From there we opened our relationship. We weren't swingers. Not at all. We would have our experiences independently. Also, there were rules. And the rules were different for both of us.

The rules for Ron Jeremy were that he had to approve with me any possibility of sex before it happened. In the case of Rio, we called it POPC: possibility of paid companionship. Also, he had to tell me all the details after. This gave me a feeling of control. My biggest fear was to be the wife in the dark. I preferred to be the wingman, the locker-room buddy (or in our case, the kitchen buddy).

Another rule was that any sex for him was to be relegated to out-of-state experiences. I made one exception, once, for a very special New York experience. With this experience, I gave him special dispensation to go in-state. But I limited the terms by giving him just two chances with which to seal the deal. I didn't want him dating her. I told him that after these two chances were up, regardless of whether he sealed the deal, it would have to be over. He sealed the deal.

The rules for me were different. I was free to do whatever I wanted with whomever I wanted (aside from, like, a mutual friend) wherever I wanted (aside from, like, our apartment). But Ron Jeremy didn't want to know about any of it. I could live my life as I so chose and have sex with whomever I chose. But I was to keep my big mouth shut. No going to Ron Jeremy for boy advice (it's hard not to do this when boys are so elusive, and your husband is a man who might have some answers). No leaving dick pics on the shared computer (oops). I had to keep it to myself.

Finally, the rules for both of us were that we always practice safe sex and always protect our love. We didn't elaborate on this last rule, the protecting of the love. But what I think it meant was: *Don't fall in love with anyone else. Don't leave me.*

The first two years that I was able, or "allowed" to be nonmonogamous, I didn't act on it. I didn't think I could handle it emotionally. I have the brain of an addict and the heart of a sixteen-year-old girl.

I remembered what I was like in my early twenties, before I'd met Ron Jeremy: attachy, pining, crushy. I felt like I wouldn't be capable of staying unattached. I would catch feels.

But after we got married, I didn't care whether I could handle it. The day after my wedding, I felt depressed. I wasn't depressed to have married Ron Jeremy. But I was depressed to be a wife. I kept having this thought that everything was over.

I don't watch romantic comedies. I didn't have the illusion that marriage means a happy ending. I knew that marriage wasn't the end of the movie. It had never really been my dream ending. But that was just it. Marriage had never really been my dream. I was not disappointed so much as confused. What did it mean to be a *wife*? The word sounded gross to me, so old and finite. I didn't want it. And so I began.

Most of the time it went like this: I would be approached by a younger man, or approach a younger man (I liked the younger ones — I already had an older one). I would let him know that I was available or interested. In my approach, I was able to be less than subtle, because having a husband gave me confidence in the face of potential rejection. If I were to be rejected immediately, I wouldn't feel like I was being rejected by all men. I had a net. Also, men really like sex. I don't think I was ever rejected.

But a problem occurred a little further in. If the sex was bad, or if I wasn't attracted to the person, I would be grossed out, kind of sad, like why am I even doing this? But if the sex was good, if the person was hot, intelligent enough for me to elevate their characteristics in my own head to talent and brilliance, then I wasn't able to just fuck and move on. I did catch feels.

There was Hunter, who was the first boy outside my marriage. Hunter taught me not to include my head in the photo when I sent nudes. That was very nice of him. I met Hunter at a holiday party. I thought he was gay, because he worked for Barneys and talked about how big his dick was. But then he said he was great at eating pussy. I was like, *Hi*.

Over the course of a month, Hunter and I made out on the street and fucked each other twice in his apartment. He had a big, crooked dick. Also, as foreshadowed, he was great at eating pussy, but I wasn't relaxed enough to come.

I obsessed about Hunter, waited for texts from him, writing a narrative in my head that he was a genius art boy (sometimes he made weird videos from his roof), when in fact he was more of an IT person with a penchant for colorful hair dye. One night I invited him to hang out and he said sorry, but he was playing video games by himself. I knew then that this was not safe for me emotionally.

Then there was Paul from creative writing class, another boy who at first I thought was gay. On the subway platform one night, I asked Paul if he had a boyfriend. Heterosexual, Paul was appalled. The next day he began doggedly pursuing me, posting on my Facebook wall the words *I'll show you hetero*. We made out in the street (I like boys who seem gay and making out in the street). He never tried to fuck me though.

Paul and I texted on and off for months. He was a disappearer. In his disappearances, I obsessed. When I confronted him about his vanishing, he said he couldn't get involved with a married woman. I don't know whether he actually was gay or was a boringly conservative straight person or just had good morals, but it wasn't going to work.

Then there was Brandon, the motorcycle boy from Long Island, who I met on cougarlife.com. I went on Cougarlife because, while I was only thirty, I think the illness made me feel older. Brandon and I rode around on his motorcycle. We also fucked in his van. I fantasized that I would move out to Long Island and tend the house, while he worked at his auto repair shop. I don't think that's what Brandon was looking for.

There was Adam, who was cute, but into Bukowski, so no.

There was Tom, who lost his virginity to me. He basically broke my vagina, but I left him with some tips on how to be gentler with the next woman.

There was Nathan, who I really liked, even though he couldn't get it up. Nathan never got a full erection yet somehow came in about fifteen seconds.

There was Matthew, who I made out with in the street to get over Nathan. Then I fell for Matthew.

There was Ben, a gorgeous twink who is actually gay. We would kiss for hours and talk about existentialism and the boy he liked in California.

In all of this, I felt like a teen — flitting between excitement and heartbreak, compulsive analysis and gameplaying. What I wanted was both my husband as well as a harem of boys who were totally devoted to me, at my beck and call at all times. That isn't really fair. Actually, it's totally fair to want it. You can want whatever you want. But the types of boys who are going to go for a woman with a husband are probably not going to be at your beck and call.

None of these experiences seemed to jeopardize my marriage in any way. If anything, they made my marriage hotter.

There is something about a long-term relationship that takes away the ability to see the other person. We stop seeing them as their own entity. We stop seeing them as a possibility, rather than a possession. Or we stop seeing the possibility of them not being there. The gap we have to cross to get to them is no longer there: the gap filled with doubt as to whether we are loved or whether he will text or whether he likes me. We stop fucking in that gap, or fucking from across that gap. We start fucking in some new shared space that we feel we own. Or maybe the shared space is still the gap but we fuck there for so long we stop seeing it.

But with an open marriage, I was consistently reminded that having sex with my husband, having a husband, was a choice. As these men were separate from me, so too was my husband. I saw them each with new eyes and was reminded that I could see my husband, each time, with new eyes.

Also, when I knew that Ron Jeremy was having sex with another woman, I would get to envision him the way another woman might envision him. I liked thinking about other women wanting him. It made me want him more.

The only experience that may have threatened my marriage was with Demetrius. He was my last lover. He was not like the other boys. Demetrius and I did not flame out quickly. We went on for a year, sexting and sending romantic emails from across the country, meeting up in hotel rooms in New York. The communication, the sex, and our connection were spiritual. I felt so connected to him, so consumed by my thoughts of him, that it made me question the truth of my marriage.

I struggled with compartmentalizing Demetrius and Ron Jeremy. It's hard to compare the person you see once every three months with the person you see every day. It's hard to compare the person you don't really know with the person you've been with for eleven years. The rarer person starts to look better. You don't see his flaws. He only shows you his best self.

Such was the case with Demetrius. I would see his most amazing side in a fantasy bubble that we constructed. Then he was gone again, and in his absence I would imagine an even more amazing Demetrius. Questions arose for me as to why what I had with Ron Jeremy didn't feel like what I felt for Demetrius. Like, why didn't my love for Ron Jeremy excite and titillate me like my new romance with Demetrius? Intellectually, I understood. But emotionally, the questions consumed me.

I think that even if I were single, it would be hard to compartmentalize my longing for Demetrius. That longing was an all-consuming longing. It made me wonder why the rest of my life, all of it, didn't sparkle like that.

Despite his request that I keep my private life private, I came clean to Ron Jeremy. I told him that I had fallen for someone. Or, as he put it, *You let your sidebitch settle in.* We decided, after five years of open marriage, to be monogamous. I didn't think I had the strength to break it off with Demetrius otherwise. If you are nonmonogamous, why would you?

It feels safer to talk openly about open marriage on this side of it. I felt that when I talked about my marriage as open, I was perceived by my straight female friends either as crazy or too idealistic or in denial. Maybe some people find it threatening — that their husbands could have desires they are not addressing. That they, themselves, might have desires that they are not addressing. That "the way things are", the status quo, doesn't have to be the way things are.

People have affairs all the time and this could be a viable alternative to monogamy. An open relationship doesn't mean all the doors fly off the things and there are no rules. It doesn't have to be an orgy. You don't have to be a 1970s swinger on a cruise ship or living on a commune in Oregon growing hemp to try this. People who look like me are trying this.

The gays, of course, understood. My gay friends

loved my open relationship. I was considered "French" and "evolved" — a beacon in the straight world. When I told my friends that Ron Jeremy and I were monogamous again, the straight ones said congratulations! The gays seemed disappointed.

I doubt that Ron Jeremy and I will be monogamous forever. Our relationship continues to evolve. Monogamy vs. open is one question that will always be up for discussion. His health may be a factor in considering whether to remain monogamous or open it up again. But it won't be the only factor.

Yes, having an open marriage can be a comfort, a defense mechanism, when I feel that my marriage, because of Ron Jeremy's health, will never look like my friends' marriages. I feel like, well okay, I can't have that. I probably wouldn't even want that, in the case of husbands and wives who do everything together, from the gym to grocery shopping. But look what I can have. But I also think that some people, like myself and Ron Jeremy, are uncomfortable with the traditional picture of marriage. Maybe we do better when we see each other simply as beloveds.

Los Angeles has been good to Ron Jeremy and me. It's easier to be a sick person in Los Angeles than in New York. LA allows for more mobility, when weakened. Also, as a sick person on the street, it's better not to have crowds of people pushing toward you. We originally moved here hoping that the weather would help him get well. While the LA sun has not been a cure, he has more of a life.

Recently, we went to a Jewish deli, where Ron Jeremy ordered an exorbitant amount of food, including a knish, which I told him not to get. The next day he complained about being fat. I was like, *I told you not to get the knish*. He said that would be a good title for an essay about marriage.

I walk into the kitchen and I kiss Ron Jeremy with an open mouth. I kiss him with an open mouth, as though he is not my husband. Or I kiss him as though he is my husband, but that the words *husband and wife* mean something else — not what I have perceived them to mean through my own fears.

In this moment I resolve to kiss my husband with an open mouth forever. I want to freeze him the way I see him in this instant: dark eyebrows, sexy, sleepy hair and sleepy eyes. But we can't freeze the way that we see the people we love, as much as we would wish. I know that I will kiss my husband with a closed mouth again, at some point. I know that I will even kiss him with a closed heart.

I pray for our love. I pray that even if I kiss my husband with a closed heart, my heart opens again to him. When I desire my husband, I am grateful to desire my husband. What can we hope for in a marriage but to keep seeing things anew? With the people we love, it is so easy to stop seeing them at all.

Under the Anxiety Is Sadness but Who Would Go Under There

I've always had general anxiety, and later came panic disorder. But it took me many years before I realized there was depression underneath the anxiety. They are the flip side of the same coin. I never identified as depressed, despite the fact that all along there was an ocean of sadness, disappointment, hopelessness, and nothingness inside me. I think the anxiety was a coping mechanism; its heightened sensations, as terrifying as they are, were in some way preferable to me than the depression underneath.

As a little kid I took fearful thoughts to a greater extreme more than most kids, I think. If a parent got sick, it was cancer. If I got something in my eye, the cornea would be scratched forever. A sprained ankle on a school trip definitely meant an amputated foot. I was dying and everyone I loved was dying, which was true, of course, but it wasn't happening as quickly as I thought.

There was no specific event that triggered the anxiety for me. Rather, the anxiety was always there, floating, looking for something to land on. Any minor event could serve as a seed, which, when nurtured with the anxiety, grew into a scary thought. The seed event would ground my fear, rendering it tangible. For someone with anxiety, dramatic situations are, in a way, more comfortable than the mundane. In dramatic situations the world rises to meet your anxiety. When there are no dramatic situations available, you turn the mundane into the dramatic.

My anxiety found a steady focus when I began having nightmares about fires at age twelve. I repeatedly dreamt that my family was burning in our home and that it was up to me to save them. Nightmares turned into daydreams and visions. I made my mother store the family's fire ladder in my bedroom and learned how to assemble it, plotting an escape route for the family out the second-floor windows. I knew how I would break the windows — the furniture that I would throw through them — should my hallucinations become a reality.

I'm not exactly sure why my anxiety chose fire to fixate on, rather than flood, hurricane, earthquake, or other myriad natural disasters. From a poetic standpoint, fire depicts passion, sexuality, and a destruction that leads to renewal. I was coming into my sexual feelings, masturbating regularly and crushing on boys, and perhaps I felt that my desires would destroy my family. Perhaps I felt ashamed.

From a nonpoetic standpoint, fire is an easy place for anxiety to live, because it is both a visually striking and painful death.

When I was thirteen, my anxiety shifted its focus to the Holocaust. As a Jewish girl, I had Holocaust images shoved down my throat from a very young age so that I would "never forget". There was the time in Hebrew school when our principal called us all into the assembly room and turned out all the lights. He then began smashing glass bottles on the ground, so as to "simulate the experience" of Krystallnacht. There was the youth group trip where the older kids locked us in a cabin and let us know the cabin was Auschwitz now and we would not be allowed to leave. Ever. There were my Zionist grandparents who warned of neo-Nazi risings in Europe. There was also Tanya, the woman who helped my mother clean the house. Tanya liked to talk about a *20/20* special she saw about the KKK. She said that the Holocaust could absolutely happen again. It could and would happen here.

I had visions of the Gestapo coming to my home. I saw my family separated. I saw my mother and father put on a train, bound for separate camps. I saw my sister and me huddled together in straw in one bunk. She was skinny and dying.

Tanya said that she would hide me when the

Holocaust came again. That was nice of her. But I was hiding from myself. I was deeply miserable about my delayed onset of puberty: my baby fat, the absence of any tits at all, my lack of menstrual cycle. Also, I was hiding from school and from my female circle of school friends, who had decided over the summer that I was no longer cool enough to be spoken to. The anxiety and friend rejection fed off each other. When I did speak to the group of my former friends, I was fearful that I was unliked. So I would say something and then laugh weirdly, right after what I said, which made me further unworthy.

Amid the loss of my friend group, the greatest heartache was the loss of my best friend. The year before, we had gotten into her father's *Playboy* magazines. We would masturbate to them together, never touching each other, but in the same room: she on the bed and me in a sleeping bag on the floor. It wasn't a sexual union that we experienced between us, but a humanistic bond: *I do this, you do this too, I'm okay, you're okay*. She even let me wear one of her bras while I masturbated, because it made me feel sexy. I didn't have my own bra yet.

But now she said that was disgusting. I was disgusting. She was over masturbation and had discovered pot and a new best friend. I didn't stop masturbating. But I felt like the only one.

In my isolation, I had this weird intuition that if I could just make it to my Bat Mitzvah I could both prevent the Holocaust from happening again and also get all my friends back. Strangely, my intuition was right.

When my Bat Mitzvah came in late fall of eighth grade, all the girls suddenly decided that I was "so cute" as to be liked again. Sometimes it takes outside advertising to frame you as "cute". An American Bat Mitzvah is just that kind of advertising. I got to make an entrance and "march in" to the song of my choosing ("Let the Sunshine In" from *Hair*). I was applauded by family and received a standing ovation. I got to "honor" my friends, who must have felt bad about no longer speaking to me, with a candle-lighting ceremony. The illusion of specialness and adolescent friendship were re-created.

The illusion of safety, as a potential Holocaust victim, was also restored. How could anything terrible come after that party? I still refused to see *Schindler's List*. But my hallucinations subsided. They say that the Bat Mitzvah is about becoming a woman. For me it was about just becoming okay again.

In high school, I channeled my anxiety into an eating disorder. Anorexia, with its counting of calories — the busyness of all that math in my head — became a wonderful place to focus my fear. Then when I was seventeen I discovered drugs and alcohol. That was the real solution.

Drugs and alcohol were the best thing that ever happened to me. For the first time, I was okay to be on the planet and completely comfortable in my own skin. Weed made my brain a playground, a new earth to be explored. Liquor, beer, and wine gave me the peace of mind I'd always sought. Psychedelics allowed me to connect with other human beings in a way where I could finally address the question of *What is going on here?* MDMA was union with these human beings in spite of the not knowing. Amphetamines kept me skinny and made me untouchable to sadness. Benzos and opiates made me impervious to the world.

I found new best friends in my substances that could protect me from my thoughts. The world became a magical place, not lonely or fearful or harsh. With my friends by my side, nobody could touch me. But then the anxiety found its way around the drugs and alcohol. Or, in the case of psychedelics and weed, it began reminding me that not only did I not know what was going on but what was going on might be more dark than benevolent. For the first time, I started getting panic attacks.

My first panic attack came shortly after I got an abortion at twenty-one. I had grown up in a household that was very liberal: socially and politically. I didn't have any hang-ups around abortion. So when I found out I was pregnant, like two days after a missed period, I called Planned Parenthood very casually.

I wanted the thing out of me as soon as possible. I had gotten pregnant by a blunt-smoking kid who ripped the sleeves off his T-shirts to make tank tops that showed his nipples. I wasn't having this kid's baby. He asked me if I would mind if he took acid on the day of the abortion.

I remember my friend Anna driving me to Planned Parenthood. I remember not being scared. I remember declining counseling. Why would I need counseling? I remember lying down on what looked like a gynecologist's table. I remember complimenting the doctor on her earrings and talking about Maine, then being administered some kind of drug. I remember going to space.

I remember coming to in a room filled with fifteen or so other women, some of them crying, some of them vomiting. I remember feeling sick and nauseous, but most of all I remember feeling fear about the sickness and nausea.

I remember getting in the car with Anna. It felt like the first time I had ever allowed myself to be vulnerable. I remember not wanting to tell any of the girls in my college house what had happened. I remember them all going out that night. I remember smoking weed and getting drunk by myself and then suddenly seeing a vision of myself going to hell. I remember not knowing where the fear had come from. I didn't even believe in hell. But the fear was there, not intellectual, but coming from someplace else. I remember seeing darkness. I remember feeling like I had crossed over a line that I could never cross back over.

A few weeks later, I went to dinner with the kid who got me pregnant and his mother. I remember her talking. I remember having food in my mouth. Suddenly, I felt like I could not swallow my food. I was scared that if I swallowed my food I would choke. I didn't know what was happening. Had I forgotten how to swallow? I wasn't sure whether to spit out the food into a napkin or keep trying to swallow. Then, in addition to being unable to swallow, I forgot how to breathe. This was my first panic attack.

Over the next few years, the panic attacks became more and more frequent. The symptoms included various combinations of dizziness, adrenaline surges, suffocation, rapid heartbeat, and the worst, a feeling of hyperreality, where people looked like plastic versions of themselves. My drinking escalated in an attempt to manage this thing that was happening to me. I didn't know that what I was experiencing were panic attacks. I just knew that every morning, ten minutes after waking up, I felt like I was dying. I would say to myself, *You felt like you were dying yesterday. But you didn't die. So even though you feel like you are dying today, you probably won't die.* But intellect couldn't refute the panic attacks.

What was happening, I later learned, was a hybrid of untreated anxiety and morning withdrawals from the same alcohol that temporarily quelled it. A psychiatrist diagnosed me with panic disorder and gave me benzodiazepines. Then I became dependent on both the benzos and the alcohol. I blacked out every night. I woke up in strange beds. My legs were covered with bruises from my blood having been so thinned by vodka. I couldn't do anything without being drunk or on pills. The thought of going to coffee with another human being while sober seemed impossible. I was either fucked up on drugs and alcohol or I felt like I was dying.

One thing that's especially sad about alcoholism and drug addiction is the way something so beautiful and sacred turns so ugly. The thing that saved my life, that made the world magical and livable, had turned on me. Alcohol and drugs worked so perfectly until they didn't work anymore. I kept trying and trying to get back to that beauty, back to the being okay.

I knew that I was tying knots that I would someday have to untie. I knew that I was going deeper and getting worse. But if you were in my head, had experienced my overwhelming feelings, you would drink too. If you felt like me, you would stay fucked up. The act of not drinking was an impossibility.

Then when I was twenty-five I got sober. I had begun practicing yoga. I didn't know it at the time, but my yoga teachers, Lisa and Yasmin, had, like, thirty years of sobriety between the two of them. I would come to class every day, high and hung over. They would smell the alcohol leaking out of my pores and gently bend me into my next pose. One day, one of them said something to me. She said, *You don't have to drink.* I was like, *Yeah right.* That was it. That was all that was said and we moved on.

A few months later I had a bad weekend. It wasn't that extreme, just sort of your usual weekend for the average twenty-five-year-old alcoholic/addict. I woke up in the bed of a person who I'd sworn I would never sleep with again. I lied to my boyfriend about my whereabouts. I dragged the person who I swore I would never sleep with again to the pharmacy. I sweated in line filling drug prescriptions. I decided to maybe only drink beer from then on. I drank a beer at eleven a.m. I started drinking liquor by evening. I got fucked up again that night. I went home in a cab at three in the morning with a bar bottle of Amstel Light in my hand. I couldn't leave it behind, because god forbid I waste any of that precious nectar. I didn't know that it would be my last drink.

The next morning I was in my teacher's yoga class again. I cannot say what happened. I only know that I heard her voice inside my head. She wasn't speaking but I heard it. I remembered what she had said to me, that I did not have to drink. I'd been called many names in my addiction: an alcoholic, cunty McDrinksalot, drunk slut. But no one had ever said it like that to me before. That I didn't have to drink. Something clicked inside me. I wondered, what if I really didn't have to drink? What about just for that day?

After yoga I went to brunch with some people. I didn't drink, which was crazy. I always drank at places where you weren't even supposed to drink. So how was it that I wasn't drinking at brunch, where drinking was sanctioned? It was the first of several miracles. The next day I didn't drink either. Or the next day.

Of course, I didn't quit everything. I continued to take pills: those prescribed to me and those not prescribed. I picked up weed again. I remember sitting by a fireplace in upstate New York, fucked up out of my mind on morphine, thinking, *This sobriety is great*.

Then, one night, I was walking home in the East Village where I lived. I passed by a church. Standing outside was a group of people, mostly gay men, smoking cigarettes. It was eight thirty on a Tuesday night. I kind of knew they weren't going to church.

I asked the men who they were. I don't know what compelled me to ask. That was the second miracle.

The men told me who they were. The third miracle is that I followed them into the church.

I have not had a drink or a drug since.

I'm not going to tell you exactly who these people were, because I'm not a spokesperson for them. I will say that they got me sober and continue to keep me sober. I will say that they are most likely in your town or city too. I think that you probably know who they are. If you can't figure it out, and you really want to know, you can email me directly at sosadtoday29@ gmail.com and I will tell you one-on-one.

After I got sober, I stopped going into withdrawal every morning and no longer felt like I was dying within twenty minutes of waking up. But my anxiety was still triggered, from time to time, by the new hyperclarity of the world. When I experienced my feelings deeply, I thought that I was going crazy. The only frame of reference I had for contextualizing emotional experiences was in terms of drugs. Now, when I felt a shift in my feelings, I could no longer attribute the change to drugs and alcohol. So I assumed either I was losing it or was dying.

I'm still very scared of my feelings and never wholly convinced that they are not going to kill me. But the panic attacks are no longer daily occurrences. Rather, they come in cycles. I'll be feeling okay for a number of months and think that I will never have one again. Then I'll have a really bad one and get scared of having more, thus triggering a cycle.

Also, I don't really get panic attacks when I'm alone anymore, only when I'm with people. My fear among people is that I will be judged for revealing what is going on inside me. I fear others will discover that I am not only imperfect; I'm not even okay. I fear that I truly am not okay. But most people who meet me never know that I am struggling. On the outside I am smiling. I am juggling all the balls of okayness: physical, emotional, mental, spiritual, existential. Underneath, I am suffocating.

One panic attack I had like this, which was almost psychedelic in nature, was the night before my wedding. I was at a dinner with my family and my soon-to-be husband's family, but my parents were late to get there. My soon-to-be mother-in-law was talking about pepper. I was going out of my mind. I just couldn't understand how this woman was talking about pepper so casually when I couldn't stop thinking about how weird it was that we were real, seated around an object, wearing cloth over our bodies, and had no idea why.

When my parents finally arrived, I took one look at them and started crying. I felt a comfort in seeing their faces that I had never felt before. I excused myself to go to the bathroom, where I wept and wept. Looking back, I think that I felt grief about leaving one stage of my life and entering a new stage. It had been more than ten years since I had lived under their roof. But there was something primal and archetypal about the transition from woman to wife. It was bigger than me.

After I cried, I felt better. I was able to return to the table and function like a human being without wondering what that meant. I think it was then that I first made the connection that underneath my anxiety was a great sadness. When I suppressed the sadness, I practically shook with existential fear over simply existing. I was fighting myself. But when the tears flowed, I felt better.

A few years later, I went through a particularly harrowing cycle of panic attacks. This one went on for months and simply wouldn't abate. I was scared that I wasn't going to be able to "keep it together". I would sit at my desk at work literally vibrating, and none of my usual fixes — the steps for combatting attacks I'd found in an ebook I'd relied on, my psychiatrist upping my meds — were working.

A friend of mine recommended that I go see a shaman she'd been working with. The idea of a New York City shaman sounded nuts. Also it cost a lot. But I was desperate. Also, I trusted this friend when she said that the work they were doing was releasing shit in her that had been blocked for years. *You can heal*, she said to me. *I used to think that I could heal a little bit or heal some things about me but not the deepest, darkest shit. But I'm discovering that you can actually really heal the worst stuff. So it's gone for good.*

The thing that scared me most about going to see the shaman was that it would be an intimate, one-on-one experience with a stranger, for many hours. At this point, my anxiety was so intense that I was scared to be one-on-one with anyone who might get close enough to me to see what was really going on. I was scared she would judge me. But I went to her little office on the Lower East Side. It was filled with stones and crystals. Also there was a cat. I was relieved by the cat, because it was something to hold.

The shaman was Irish. She asked me some questions about how I'd been feeling, physically. I told her that right at that moment, I felt like the area from my rib cage to my neck was going to explode. It wasn't a heart attack–type sensation. More like a balloon full of mourning. I could not say what I was mourning.

The shaman said, *That doesn't sound like anxiety to me. It sounds like depression.*

Then she turned off the lights and said some prayers. She spoke with some of the archangels. She asked me to close my eyes and to speak to them as well. I was like, *What the fuck?* But I was paying a lot, so I did it.

I chose the archangel Michael. I didn't know anything about him. To this day I don't particularly feel that attached to him. He was just the one who came into my head.

She asked if Michael could go down into my body. I was like, *Okay.* She asked me to go with him. She asked me to report what I saw. She also said to suspend any doubts I might have about possession or being inhabited by foreign bodies or beings. She said we all contain foreign bodies or beings — things that are not ours and not our soul within us. She said we sometimes pick them up from other people. Like there are things we are taught that aren't ours.

Or they are curses. She said that every time a parent yells at a child that it is a curse.

The shaman, Michael, and I found a bat, two rats, and a shield-shaped being inside the walls of my sternum. She asked Michael to give them a boat to heaven so they could leave me.

The bat and the rats left easily. They hadn't even known they were inside me. The shield-shaped being, I discovered, was passed down from my father's family. He was full of biting sarcasm and believed he was there to protect me. The shield-shaped being was trying to protect my soul orb, a snow-globe-type thing that lived behind my rib cage. The problem was that while the shield-shaped being was protecting me from hurt, no light could get in either.

The shaman talked to the shield-shaped being in shield language, which turned out to be English. She let him know I was not his home and gave him permission to leave me. He cried as he left my body.

The shaman said I was now vacant of beings. She said my core would not stay empty. I would repopulate with me.

When I left the shaman I felt like I could breathe again. But I didn't feel like that for long. I can't say whether the bats, rats, and shield I saw were real or unreal. Like, I think what I saw were archetypes. I think I entered a hypnotic place between sleep and waking where you can suspend your disbelief. But if the shaman is right — that the ideas and pains we acquire from outside ourselves are actual beings — then I think she missed some. I still feel very much populated by them.

One thing that the shaman gave me was the ability to call what I was feeling depression. I had never called it that before. When I told my psychiatrist about the shaman, I was like, *She said I had depression.* The psychiatrist was like, *Oh yes, you definitely do.* I was like, *Um, it would've been cool if you had said something to me before.* I guess she thought I knew that when we spoke of my anxiety we were also speaking of depression.

I was still struggling a lot, particularly at work. But I did find something else that helped a little bit. When I felt like I was dying, I began tweeting anonymously from an account that I called @sosadtoday. I was mostly tweeting into the abyss. I followed, like, three people who I had admired on weird Twitter but who I didn't follow from my personal Twitter account. That was it.

But there was something about the visceral impact of sending what I was feeling out into the universe that felt different than just writing in a journal. It gave me relief. Maybe it was just the dopamine of hitting Send, but I felt like things were starting to move and clear out of me. Then people started following, in rapid numbers. The account grew and grew.

Then a really weird thing happened. I began to come out of my all-consuming anxiety and depression. But what I found was that there were always daily sadnesses to tweet about. I had never acknowledged this before, how sad things were. I guess I had always felt that to admit to myself that I was sad meant it was real. It made me feel like a loser. Who wants to be sad? But all of those sadnesses, unacknowledged over time, were pushing up against the Band-Aids I put over them. As anxiety and depression, they were screaming to get out.

As I mined my feelings for the account, which grew bigger and bigger, I felt like the opposite of a loser. I felt popular. I felt popular based on my truth. I began to celebrate this sensitive part of me — the things that I thought were most despicable: my need for constant validation, disappointment, feeling gross and fat and ugly. Also more essential things like, Why are we here? And what's the point? The more real I was, the more people could relate. It seemed like there were a shitload of people who were scared of life and death, also people who were disappointed when they tried to partake in activities to cover over these fears and the activities didn't work out, and they were forced once again to return to their primal sadnesses.

There were other Twitter accounts in this vein that seemed stupid to me. There were accounts where people were saying, *If you're depressed or sad, just get up and dance.* That's a crazy fucking thing to tell a depressed person. I felt that in the reality of what I had experienced, it was a lot more helpful to just lie there and share experiences with others who understood. What worked for me was to maybe make myself laugh about my plight, and through the grace of the Internet, make other people laugh.

The experience of being alive, its *is*ness, maybe in relation to the future *isn't*ness of death or maybe independent of that, or maybe a hybrid of both, can hurt so much sometimes. Sometimes it still hurts so much to be alive that I want to die. I am scared of dying and sad about dying and that is part of the hurt.

Why aren't we all walking around and acknowledging this all the time? Maybe we can't afford to. Maybe when we're not in the fear and sadness, we run from it. We don't want to think about it.

I know I have an ocean of sadness inside me and I have been damming it my entire life. I always imagined that something was supposed to rescue me from the ocean. But maybe the ocean is its own ultimate rescue — a reprieve from the linear mind and into the world of feeling. Shouldn't someone have told me this at birth? Shouldn't someone have said, "Enjoy your ocean of sadness, there is nothing to fear in it," so I didn't have to build all those dams? I think some of us are less equipped to deal with our oceans, or maybe we are just more terrified, because we see and feel a little extra. So we build our shitty dams. But inevitably, the dam always breaks again. It breaks again and the ocean speaks to me. It says, *I'm alive and it's real*. It says, *I'm going to die and it's real*.

With a name like So Sad Today, I feel pressure to write the perfect essay about anxiety and depression. But it's the illusion of perfection that catalyzes my anxiety and depression. Perfectionism turns a minor shift in body temperature, a missed breath, into a full-fledged panic attack, especially when I am in the company of people for whom I feel I need to perform. The beginnings of a panic attack — the shortness of breath, the tightness in my chest, the unreality — are simply sensations. They will escalate or dissolve based on how fearfully I respond to them. Thus far, I've usually responded fearfully.

Perfectionism, of course, is not the sole culprit in my anxiety and depression. There is also chemistry, sensitivity, history, nurture, DNA, and questions existential and mystic — questions I have been discouraged from thinking about too hard, like, *Why am I here? What is all of this? Am I going to die? Am I going to die right now? If I die right now, is that all there is? If I don't die right now, is this all there is?*

It seems weird to me that here we are, alive, not knowing why we are alive, and just going about our business, sort of ignoring that fact. How are we all not looking at each other all the time just like, *Yo, what the fuck?*

In the name of perfectionism, I have tried to stick to a linear narrative in describing my history of anxiety and depression, as it is a trajectory that most of us can follow in our surface comings and goings. Hopefully I was able to transcend it just a little. Maybe you relate to my *what the fuckness* and feel a little better about your own. All I want from you is to be liked. Of course, that is a scared woman's way of saying what I really want, which is to connect with you on a deep and true level while I am still on this earth, and maybe even after I am off it.

Acknowledgments

Love and thanks to:

Sara Weiss, for bringing me on
Karah Preiss, for moving and shaking
Meredith Kaffel Simonoff, for being more than an agent
Libby Burton, for edits on fleek
Jonathan Smith, for VICE cool and unexpected kindness
The first SST followers, for finding me in a dark corner of
the Internet
THE TEENS, I love you most of all!!! <3 <3 <3
Liz Pelly, Jenn Pelly, Brandon Stosuy, Gabby Bess, James
Montgomery, Preteen Gallery, Hazel Cills, Nimrod
Kamer, Simon Vozick-Levinson, Safy Hallan-Farrah, Sky
Ferreira, and Dev Hynes, for blowing my shit up
Brad Listi, for dreaming big. Bush did 9/11. #chalupa
Caitlin Mulrooney-Lyski, for publicizing a publicist
Carolyn Kurek, best copyedits ever
Roxane Gay, Jami Attenberg, Molly Crabapple, and
Bethany Cosentino for being lovely and early responders
Geoff Kloske, for Meredith (and also just being nice)
Kristen Iskandrian and Lorian Long, for witchin' out

Tyler Crawford, ilysm bae

Hayley, for going through it all with me, I love you

Mom and Dad, I love you (and sorry)

Nicky, for the comprehensive love package and keeping it the most real

Some names and identifying details have been changed to protect the privacy of others. Thanks to *VICE* and *The Fanzine*, where some of the material in *So Sad Today* first appeared in a different form.